EVERYDAY

My Absolute Best for My King

EVERYDAY

My Absolute Best for My King

Contemplations On the Love of God

RONALD T. HICKEY

HICKEY HOUSE BOOKS

Published by Hickey House Books

EVERYDAY
My Absolute Best for My King
Contemplations on the Love of God
Copyright © 2024 by Ronald T. Hickey

For information address: Hickey House Books, 1079 Sunrise Ave, Ste. B-205, Roseville, CA 95661. Trademarks appearing in the book are the property of their respective owners and are used only to identify them and/or their products and services.

EVERYDAY: My Absolute Best for My King™ is a trademark owned by Ronald T. Hickey
Printed in the United States of America.
10 9 8 7 6 5 4 3 2 1
ISBN 978-1-966007-02-9
Editor: Dr. Rosalind Robinson
Hickey House Books
Roseville, California 95661
www.hickeyhousebooks.com

For My King

TABLE OF
CONTENTS

Introduction

CONTEMPLATING THE LOVE OF GOD

*"For God so loved the world that he gave his
one and only Son, that whoever believes in
him shall not perish but have eternal life."*

—*JOHN 3:16 (NIV)*

Believing Jesus lived, was crucified, buried, resurrected on the third day, and ascended to the Right Hand of the Throne of God is the basic of Christian belief. As saints, we must move beyond believing in our basic beliefs and seeking the living God in the spirit of knowing. This life is a real struggle, every day, and we must live in a manner that demonstrates that we believe with every ounce of our being that Jesus, as surely has He rose from His earthly grave, is going to return one day. Do we really contemplate the return of Jesus Christ? Do we contemplate the Love of God in His singular act of giving the life of His One and only Son? God sent Jesus to give His life so we could have eternal life. Jesus went to prepare a place for His followers. Therefore, He is coming back, and since He is coming back, what is He coming back for? Or better yet, who is He coming back for? The only manner by which we can honor His return and the Love of God and ensure we are in the procession of saints on Judgement Day is by giving our absolute best to our King, every day. This book, EVERYDAY, My Absolute Best for My King, is a collection of my daily contemplations that pull me closer into my relationship with the King. In contemplating the Love of God, this book's true value to the saint rests in its overbearing insistence that Jesus, because of the reality of the tragedy on the Cross, through the redemptive power of His life, death, and resurrection, is the only secure foundation upon which a Christian can resurrect a life in Christ and be made whole and held blameless. If Jesus returned today, are you living in a manner by which God would hold you blameless? Has the Holy Ghost made you whole in the life of Christ? Have you given Christ your absolute best? Christ gave His life for yours. Are you giving your life to Him? This book not only insist that we must give our lives to Christ, be broken bread and poured out wine, but it also helps us understand how to give our lives back to Christ, every day!

EVERYDAY will bring you back to Jesus Christ, where your spirit should rest every moment of every day and guide you to having much deeper contemplations in your walk with the King. God loves us and calls us to come higher. Don't be basic in your belief. Contemplate the Love of God and give your absolute best to our King! EVERDAY!

This book is the first in a series of 4 books. Each of the books will present 13 weeks of deep contemplations, a journey of sort, focused on (1) the Love of God, (2) the Glory of God, (3) the Nature of God, and (4) the Promises of God; respectively. The series is designed in a manner that allows saints to focus their needs around a singular aspect of God or allows saints to gain a broader understanding of God by reading the entire series. I do not offer the series from the perspective of a theologian, because I am not a theologian. I have not studied theology and attended the seminary, but I have studied the word of God extensively, and I am gifted with the gifts of wisdom and discernment. Each contemplation derives from my own personal experiences with the Living God. I am not one who believes God and Christ exist; I know They exist. God and Christ have moved in my life in mighty, mighty ways. Therefore, I am no longer a believer; I know! I know God exists. I know Jesus Christ exists. I know the Holy Ghost is real.

While my contemplations are influenced by all Christian religious books, sermons, and text, including the Bible and daily devotionals, I have read and/or listened to over the years, the contemplations in this series of books are not meant to be an interpretation of any other book, sermon, or text. These contemplations are depictions of my personal understandings. I have attempted to bring my Christian journey to life in a manner that allows all saints to gain a deeper understanding of our Lord and Savior so you can come to know Him for yourself. The great command unto all saints of the Living God is to spread the gospel to all nations. EVERYDAY is my act of obedience to the great command. I pray the words of my mind, and the mediations of my heart, will, in some great manner, bring each saint into a deeper, more meaningful, and richer relationship with God and the Redemptive Power of Jesus Christ. May your lifelong journey into the depths of the love, nature, glory, and promises of the Lord begin today and continue EVERYDAY!

EVERYDAY
CHRIST JESUS

*"…So that now as always Christ will be
exalted in my body, whether by life or death.
For to me, to live is Christ and to die is gain."*

—*Philippians 1:20-21 (NIV)*

My Absolute Best for My King. "I eagerly expect and hope that I will in no way be ashamed." (Verse 20). We must hold our thoughts captive and yield our every human desire to the will of God; until we make our every action obedient to Christ Jesus. We must do this in every moment of each day, or we will feel very much ashamed on the very issue to which Christ Jesus has asked us to surrender to His will. As Paul directs, we must exalt Christ Jesus every day in our body, whether in life or death. Irrespective of time and circumstance, I must give my absolute best to my King, everyday! To get to this point, by no stretch of the imagination, is not easy; for it comes by complete, absolute, and unequivocal surrender to the will of Christ Jesus. Surrendering is not a product of conscience thought or debate. There is no amount of reasoning or making sense of surrendering. Surrendering your will to God's will comes only by spiritual obedience to the truths of God that lead you to seek nothing but God Himself. To exalt Christ in my body, whether by life or death, means I have irrevocably surrendered my will to the purpose for which God has made me; including living or dying for my King, in every moment of every day. You cannot partially surrender. You cannot yield up to a certain point. With Christ, you are either all in or all out. You can't love Christ one day and feel ashamed the next. You must feel as Paul did; "To live is Christ." We can have no consideration for ourselves or the well-being of others. God does not care about the circumstances of our lives. He only cares that we are willing to say; "Lord! God Almighty! I am nothing without you! Have your way with my life." We cannot debate with God that surrendering our will to Him will bring harm to our spouse, children, mother, father, brother or sister. I must give my absolute best to my King, every day, without considering who may be harmed. God will care for the well-being of the ones I love. I must love Him first, above all else. I must seek Him first; even before I seek His blessings and rewards. Everyday, in my life or death, I must be able to look at my every circumstance and see the face of God. If I see anything else, other than Jesus, in my sadness and sorrow, in my joy and happiness, in my wants and desires, in my blessings and rewards, then I risk feeling ashamed of my King. I must be determined to be *"My Absolute Best for My King."*

My Undying Commitment to My King. "For it has been granted to you on behalf of Christ not only to believe in Him, but also to suffer for Him." (Verse 29). Whether it means life or death, we must be determined to allow nothing to keep us from being rightly related to the life, death, resurrection and ascension of Christ Jesus. Our commitment to His commandments and His great commission must be undying. It is not enough to simply believe that Christ died on the cross; we must be willing to suffer with Him on His Cross. I must be willing to suffer every day for my King. God's order of commitment to Him may sometimes work up a storm of uncertainty, strife or struggle in our lives. Suffering produces perseverance, perseverance character, and character hope. There is the "hope" in, "I eagerly expect and hope I will not be ashamed." This is the "character" that produces my undying commitment to my King, every day. When the suffering has found you, in your belief in Christ, that is the very moment in which you must make an undying commitment to giving your absolute best to your King; each and every day!

GOING OUT BY FAITH

*"By faith Abraham, when called to go
to a place he would later receive as his
inheritance, obeyed and went, even though
he did not know where he was going."*

—*Hebrews 11:8 (NIV)*

A new year, a new beginning, and a new opportunity can create feelings of excitement as well as uncertainty. In many circumstances we are more than willing to leave the past, the old and the routine, for the new year; a fresh start or an anticipated chance to do something we have always wanted to do. When we look back, we can find delight, but we can also see the pain, hurt and suffering. So, we are more than ready to look toward tomorrow or the new year or a new beginning. God has made some promises, and we look to new opportunities in hopes of receiving the promises we have been hoping for. The promises of God are always on the way, but we must be willing to obey and go where God sends us, even though we may not know where we are going. We go into the new year not really knowing what the new year will bring. We may begin new employment or start a new relationship not really knowing what they will bring. We oftentimes go "out" not knowing. Have you gone "out" by faith, as Abraham did? If so, there is no logical reason for your going out, other than trusting in God. We don't have the answers to the questions we ask; God does. We have no idea what the new day will bring, or who we may meet in the new place we have "went" to. Abraham "obeyed and went" to a place that he would later learn was the land God had promised him. One of the more challenging tasks in Christian work is obeying and going out by faith not knowing what to expect. Have you gone out into the new year by faith not knowing what to expect? Sure, you are full of hope, belief and trust; but do you really know what to expect? Did you expect everything that happened last year? Did you expect all that happened in the last place you "went" to? Did you expect all that transpired with the last person you trusted? We really don't know what to expect; all we know "by faith" is that God knows what He is doing and what He is going to do in our lives. In the newness of tomorrow, the new year, a new opportunity, and a new destination, we must constantly adjust our attitude toward our expectations of God. Never anticipate what God is going to do. Wait on the instructions of the Lord; obey Him without doubt or hesitation and go by faith where He says go. "Do not consider your life, not even for a moment." This attitude keeps you continually excited. You don't know what God is going to do, but you do know He is going to do something.

Have you been praying to God, asking Him to reveal His plan for you? Stop waiting for His answer; it is not coming. God does not reveal His plan; He only reveals Himself to us. We should only seek God Himself, and all else will be given unto us, in accordance to God's will and His time. His promises may not be delivered in this new year, in a new opportunity, in the next day or in the next place we go to. Do not anticipate when God will act. Seek only the kingdom of God with no expectation of anything other than God Himself. Surrender your will, anticipation and expectation, until you are no longer excited about what God may do tomorrow. God is the God you believe He is. *"Therefore, I tell you, do not worry about your life, what you will eat or drink, or about your body, what you will wear."* (Matthew 6:25 NIV). Your only concern should be "Going out by Faith" and ensuring there is no space in your heart between your love for God in Christ and God's love, mercy, goodness, grace, kindness, and His promises to you.

Week 1 Day 3

LIGHT AND JOY

*"Light is shed upon the righteous and
joy on the upright in heart."*

—PSALMS 97:11 (NIV)

"I was young and now I am old, yet I have never seen the righteous forsaken." (Psalm 37:25 NIV). Until you are born of the Spirit of God, you may believe the teachings and commands of Jesus Christ are simple and easy. But once you have been born again of the Spirit, you quickly learn that living in accordance to the teachings of Christ is no fairytale. *"Clouds and thick darkness surround him."* (Psalms 97:2). Once we make the decision to follow Jesus and draw closer to His perfect character, we learn just how difficult it is to follow His teachings, and we find that His commands on our lives come with clouds and thick darkness. But God says He will not forsake the righteous. We may experience clouds and dark days, but God's "light is shed upon the righteous and joy on the upright in heart." Whether you are young or old, God will not forsake a righteous soul with an upright heart. The teachings of Christ provide us the first insight into the aspects of righteous living for the Lord. The understanding of the teachings of Jesus comes by the light the Holy Spirit shines within us, not by the dark clouds outside of us.

Righteousness and an upright heart are not common-place religious experiences, and until you realize that Christ does not dwell in your commonplace thinking, but in your surrender and your faith in God, you cannot get to the presence of God in your circumstances. Until you get beyond the elementary notion of God only as a deliverer of blessings, you will never be able to look into the clouds and see through the thick darkness of your circumstances and witness the face of God. Those who approach God with doubt and hesitation, with basic wants and personal interests, have not been introduced to the Atonement of Jesus Chris; and they do not know the Redemptive Power of the Holy Spirit. After the tantaliz-ing delight and freedom of volition in acknowledging what Jesus Christ has done, comes the undeniable joy in the light and truth of knowing Who Christ is. "Jesus is the light in my darkness and the joy in my heart."

Jesus said, *"I am the way and the truth and the life. No one comes to the Father except through me,"* (John 14:6) and *"I am the light of the world. Whoever follows me will not walk in darkness, but will have the light of life."* (John 8:12). The Bible is just great sounding words that we read, until Jesus speaks them into us in a particular spiritual manner that only He can; then the words become living spirit and eternal life. God does not shed His light or give us His joy through dreams of light or visions of joy; He sheds His light and imparts His joy by the words and teachings of His Son, Christ Jesus, our Lord and Savior. Jesus is the "way" and the "truth" and the "life." Through Christ Jesus, the clouds and the thick darkness are turned into light and joy that lead to life. No one comes to the Father expect through Jesus, and the clouds and thick darkness that surround Him. When we get to God it is by the words and teachings of Christ. We cannot avoid the dark days, but we can follow the commands of the word of Christ to live righteously and holy. If you keep this command, God said; "you will never be forsaken."

Week 1 Day 4

YOU WILL FOLLOW LATER

"Where I am going, you cannot follow now, but you will follow later."

—*John 13:36 (NIV)*

"*For the Lord will go before you.*" (Isaiah 52:12 NIV). We must wait patiently on the Lord. There are situations in which Christ must go and prepare a place for us. God knows best, and He seldom reveals His plan to us. We may desire to follow Jesus as soon as He goes, but He simply says; "You will follow later." Christ Jesus goes ahead of us and clears the path of righteousness for His name's sake, removing those things that could otherwise cause us to doubt our salvation. While working on our behalf, God may go completely silent. When God goes silent, that is a sign to be still and wait, not to attempt to fill in the silence with your own thoughts or self-interest. God's silence may have come to teach you what it really means to trust in the Lord. Perhaps God's silence has come so you may learn what it means to suffer with Christ in service. Never strike out on your own. Wait to hear from God. If there is any doubt or hesitation, then God has not spoken. Wait on God until you are sure you are sure; and when you are sure, that is the precise time to follow Christ.

Doing the will of God requires patience. Initially you may believe God has sent you a clear message concerning what He wants you to do. It may seem clear that He is signaling you to separate from your mother or father, your friend or brother, or from your sister or colleague. It may even be clear that God is directing you to separate from your spouse or children. God may be severing a business relationship, or breaking you away from a ministry you started, or something else you feel distinctly clear that it is of God's will for you to do. Never do such things on the impulse of a whim arising out of your own human instinct or will. Because you have one foot out of a situation does not mean God is telling you to take both feet out. "You will follow later." If you act too soon or impulsively, regret will surely follow, and it may take years to repair the damage you may have caused to yourself and others. If you operate on God's timeline, there will be no broken hearts, no regret, no resentment and no lingering ill feelings. When we do not have the patience to wait on God and attempt to fill in the silence with our own self-guided impulses, we create an enormous amount of grief, despair, and disappointment.

Don't be like Peter! Peter was wholly impatient. He anticipated and developed unsubstantiated expectations that led him to fail the test as a result. Peter did not expect to deny Jesus three times before the rooster crowed. Peter did not even know himself as well as Jesus knew him. Jesus knew Peter would deny Him. Peter could not follow Jesus because he did not know himself well enough to ensure how he would respond to any given situation. God will never give you the signal to follow if He knows you do not know yourself well enough to figure out how you will respond when the crisis comes. Peter's lack of knowledge of himself was the result of his lack of spiritual devotion to Christ. Peter loved Christ in a natural sense, but Peter lacked spiritual knowledge of Christ, thus lacked knowledge of himself in relation to Christ. That is why he and the other disciples could not yet follow Jesus. It was not until Jesus rose from the dead and the Holy Spirit was given up unto the disciples that they were ready to serve the Lord. We must come to know God through the grace of the Holy Spirit residing in us, then we can follow Jesus.

Week 1 Day 5

THE POWER OF THE HOLY SPIRIT

"Again Jesus said, 'Peace be with you!
As the Father has sent me, I am sending
you.' And with that He breathed on them
and said, 'Receive the Holy Spirit.'"

—*John 20:21-22 (NIV)*

Following Christ can be an easy endeavor when you are caught up in the hype and the fascination that surrounds the Son of God. We become star-stricken with a silly fascination and idolization. So, when Jesus called the twelve disciples, they gladly followed Jesus and the celebrity-like lifestyle that was upon Him. The disciples traveled around the country with Jesus, relishing in the fanfare that Jesus attracted. They did not need the Holy Spirit to help them follow Christ Jesus; they were mesmerized by Jesus, and would follow Him anywhere, just to be next to such a phenomenal figure. But, like Peter, one of the twelve, when your connection to Christ is only a natural, human fascination guided by mesmerized human emotions, you stand the chance of denying Jesus when put to the right test. Peter was tested three times, and he denied Jesus three times. Peter became distraught, because He really did love Jesus, and he could not imagine denying Jesus. But he did. Then Jesus breathed on Peter and the other disciples and said, "Receive the Holy Spirit." When you receive the Power of the Holy Spirit there is nothing fascinating or mesmerizing about life anymore. Life becomes real, and with the Power of the Holy Spirit imparted into you, Jesus says once again, "Follow Me!"

Before the death of Christ, the disciples could follow Christ wherever He was going. *"Where I am going, you cannot follow now, but you will follow later."* (John 13:37 NIV). Once Jesus rose, they could not follow Him where He was going, which was to sit on the right-hand of the Throne of God. You can easily follow Jesus when the fascination of Him is upon you. Your first call to "Follow Me" is an external proposition that does not involve the imparting of the Holy Spirit. The second calling, after you have received the Holy Spirit, is an internal appeal to "Follow Me" in total surrender of your mind, body and spirit, in life or in death. *"When you are old you will stretch out your hands, and someone else will dress you and lead you where you do not want to go."* (John 21:18 NIV). "Jesus said this to give an indication of the kind of death by which Peter would glorify God." (Verse 19). After Jesus described to Peter how Peter would die, He then told Peter a second time to, "Follow Me!" Peter had to totally surrender to the will of the Lord.

God bring us to the very end of our intellect, talents, abilities, and self-sufficiency; He brings us to the very end of our knowledge and awareness. God brings us to His knowledge, the knowledge that we are nothing without Him. God alone decides how we live and die. God brings us to the point where we realize we cannot rely on anything but God; not even the fascination of Christ will save us; only the Power of the Holy Ghost. When we get to this level of realization, where we are completely destitute and poor in spirit, we are then perfectly conditioned to receive from Christ Jesus the impartation of the Power of the Holy Spirit. When we know that we cannot rely on anything other than the Lord Jesus Christ and the Spirit that only He can breathe into us, we are then ready to answer His second call to, "Follow Me!" We have no power to guide our own lives with our meaningless vows, devotions and resolutions. There is only one North Star by which our lives should be guided, the Lord Jesus Christ; and that is only after He has invaded our spirit with the Power of the Holy Spirit.

Week 1 Day 6

WORSHIP, WAIT AND WORK

*"The Lord had said to Abram, 'Leave
your country, your people and your father's
household and go to the land I will show you.'"*

—GENESIS 12:1 (NIV)

Worship is forfeiting your right to yourself and giving back to God everything He has given to you in spiritual praise. You must appreciate and be a steward over the blessings from God, being careful not to squander your gifts and to avoid doing meaningless things. God Almighty Himself should be the primary beneficiary of everything He has blessed you with, your talent, intellect, spirit and perfect character. Your day should begin and end worshipping God with praise and thanks. You should go about your day worshipping God with your work and showing patience to wait on Him. Your act of worship should be generous, purposefully and deliberate, giving back to God what He has blessed you with. Like Abraham, you must worship God with your words of praise, captive thoughts, acts of obedience and patient waiting. You must give everything God has given you back to God, or risk spiritual ruin. God's gifts to you are not meant to be hoarded and stored away for safe keeping. (Matthew 25:14-29 *The Parable of the Talents*). God's blessings are like money, they should be invested in accordance to God's will and His purpose for your life. When you invest God's blessings, He is able to receive it back in greater abundance and bless others with His gains. *"Well then, you should have put my money on deposit with the bankers, so that when I returned I would have received it back with interest."* (Matthew 25:27 NIV). Remember what happened to the manna when it was hoarded and stored away, instead of being made available as a blessing for others? The manna rotted and became unsafe for human consumption. How many of your blessings from God have you hoarded and ruined because you did not put the blessing to good use? How many of your talents did God take away from you, because you were not putting the talent to the best use in accordance to God's will and purpose in giving you the talent? Whatever God gives to you, whether it is a little or a lot, you must put it to good use. You must invest it smartly and wait on God to take it back so that He can reinvest the blessing for the sake of others. If you hoard something God has given to you, you prevent God from being able to bless others. That is precisely why God will not allow you to hoard His gifts. If you do, He will take those gifts from you and give them to someone else who has proven to be a good steward of the blessings He has given them.

When you obey God and go where He tells you to go, that is a symbol of communion with God and worshipping Him with your obedience. God may send you anywhere throughout the world. Like His faithful servant Abraham, you should remain prepared to move quickly. That's why Abraham pitched no more than a tent. Abraham's focus was worship, waiting and working, as a servant of God. Abraham did not hoard; he did not have a big house or a big barn to store things. *"So you knew that I harvested where I have not sown and gather where I have not scattered seed?"* (Matthew 25:26 NIV). The measure of our worth to God is what we give back to God in communion. We are His workers in the field. We are to sow the seed and take in the harvest for God so He can bless others. We cannot rush the work of God, and we cannot rush worshipping God. Our tents must be pitched in a place that will allow us to get quiet and worship God in quiet patience, waiting for Him to guide us to His harvest, which we gather for Him. Worshiping, waiting, and working are to be done simultaneously in the spirit, not separately in natural phases. It is a process we have to learn through spiritual discipline. In the life of our Lord, Jesus Christ, worshiping, waiting and working were simultaneous acts of the Redeemer.

IF YOU REMAIN IN THE LOVE OF CHRIST

"As the Father has loved me, so have I loved you. Now remain in my love."

—*JOHN 15:9 (NIV)*

"*I am the vine; you are the branches. If a man remains in me and I in him, he will bear much fruit.*" (Verse 5). When you come into the intimate knowledge of Jesus Christ, will you love him? Will you remain in His Love? There is no guarantee that you will love Christ. There is no guarantee that you will even get to know Him intimately enough to consider His love. The Disciples walked with Jesus every day, yet they denied Him in the end and did not know Him as intimately as they eventually would. This is precisely why Jesus says, "If you remain." Christ does not know what man will do with the volition God has given us. We must choose righteousness. We must choose Christ. We must choose to remain in His love. We must choose to remain a branch in Christ the vine. And "if" we do we "will bear much fruit." Christ tells us we have a blessing coming "if we remain in Him." The word "if" is a proposition and is not used to rebuke you or even meant to be a surprise to anyone. Jesus knows the soul of man better than we know ourselves. The word "if" is used as a leading proposition to suggest that there is a great reward waiting "if" we do a specific thing. In the case of verse 5, we will bear much fruit if we remain a branch in Christ the vine. If we do something that Jesus Christ commands, He will deliver what He has promised He would.

"If you remain in me and my words remain in you, ask whatever you wish, and it will be given you." (Verse 7). God is a generous God. The Lord Almighty's desire is that all of His people thrive and live extravagantly well, giving Him all the glory and praise. But there are some requirements, some specific expectations to gaining access to the blessings of the Father, that come through the name of Jesus Christ. Whatever we wish for, Jesus promises He will give to us, "if" we remain in Him, and "if" His word remains in us. Again, the word "if" is a leading proposition that suggests there is

a blessing that is associated with our obedience to the commands of Christ. (See the Beatitudes, Matthews 5:1-12). All of the blessings promised in the Beatitudes are dependent upon a specific obedience to a command given by Christ Jesus. "Blessed are the pure in heart for they will see God."

"If you obey my commands, you will remain in my love, just as I have obeyed my Father's commands and remain in his love." (Verse 10). The love of Jesus comes from an intimate relationship with Christ that is derived from a type of friendship that is rare on earth. Rare friendships are abased in a level of rare obedience to a shared set of principles. Remember the friends you had when you were eight years old? You shared an intimate identity in and an obedience to a particular thought, heart and spirit with your childhood friends. We keep those friends for life if we are able to remain in intimate identity in and obedience to a particular thought, heart, and spirit into adulthood. If we lose such identities with our friends, the friendship slowly dies off. This is precisely the type of friendship involved in the love of Christ. We must intimately identify with Christ in thought, in heart and in spirit. If we do this specific thing, obeying the commands of Christ Jesus, then He said we will remain in His love; bearing much fruit and receiving whatever we wish to ask for. Obedience to the Lord is the ultimate expression of love.

Week 2 Day 1

THE LOVE OF CHRIST

*"My command is this: Love each
other as I have loved you."*

—John 15:12 (NIV)

"*Greater love has no one than this, that he lay down his life for his friends.*" (Verse 13). Christ Jesus gave His life so that we might be justified before God and have access to the kingdom. There is no greater love than the love Jesus has shown mankind; and all He asks in return is that we love each other as He has loved us and for us to do what He commands. *"You are my friends if you do what I command."*

(Verse 14). Are you a friend to Jesus? Do you do what He commands? To do what Jesus Christ commands is to enter into an intimate friendship with Christ. Once we get intimate with Jesus we are never alone again; we have a constant companion Who will never leave our side. Because of the love of Christ, we never need the sympathy or empathy of others; we can be transparently vulnerable with our thoughts, heart, and spirit without being judged or ridiculed. Jesus does not tear down His friends, He builds us up in His image, imparting His perfect character. When the love of Christ abides in you, you will never leave impressions of yourself or consider your expectations with anticipation; you will only give God the glory by surrendering to Jesus Christ and allowing Him to have His unrestricted way with your life. The farthest regions of your thoughts, heart, and spirit will be completely satisfied by the love of Christ. When you have reached this level of intimacy with Christ Jesus, the only expressions of your nature will be that of a saint who is faithfully walking beside the still waters. You will have no worries, because you know you can trust in the love of Christ. Heartache and pain? No worry! Sadness and hurt? No worry! Unemployment and no friends? No worry! Trials and tribulations? No worry! Jesus loves you!

"You did not choose me, but I chose you and appointed you to go and bear fruit—fruit that will last." (Verse 16). Disciples of Christ do not choose Christ, He chooses His disciples and appoints His disciples to go and bear fruit, "to make saints of all nations." We can have a wonderful, intimate relationship

with Jesus; but there is a greater, much closer intimacy to be had with the Lord. The initial intimacy is a natural inclination to connect with the splendor of Christ in the nature of a fan who follows his or her idol. The greater much closer intimacy with Christ comes when Christ breathes on you and imparts the Holy Spirit into your soul. When this happens, you are no longer a fanatic follower of Christ, but a friend who intimately identifies with spirit, heart and thoughts of Christ. *"I no longer call you servants, because a servant does not know this master's business. Instead, I have called you friends, for everything that I learned from my Father I have made known to you."* (Verse 15). The first level of intimacy with Christ is that of service, and the greater, much closer intimacy is that of friendship. The whole purpose of life is to engage Christ Jesus in this closest intimacy of friendship, and to do what Jesus commands, expressing only a strong calm of love for Christ and others, just as Christ loves us. Do you have the love of Christ?

We are quick to ask for the blessings, rewards and promises, but are we intimate with Our Lord Jesus Christ? Are we His friends? It is an absolute delight to Jesus when a disciple whom He has chosen and appointed to go and bear fruit takes the time to get closer and more intimate with Him. Bearing fruit that will last is the true manifestation of an intimate relationship between you and Christ.

OPEN YOUR EYES AND RECEIVE

"To open their eyes and turn them from darkness to light, and from the Power of Satan to God, so that they may receive forgiveness of sin and a place among those who are sanctified by faith in me."

—ACTS 26:18 (NIV)

This verse, more than any other in the entire Bible, describes the enormous call on the life of a servant of Jesus Christ. This verse gives a disciple of Christ his or her charge; to open the eyes of others so that they may receive.

"Open your eyes and receive" is also the charge on the individual seeking the kingdom of God. It is the absolute sovereign work of God's grace that we are able to receive forgiveness of our sins. When we fall short of the full Christian experience it is because we have not received remission of sins; we have not been saved by the grace of God through Christ Jesus. As disciples of Christ, we are called to lead others to salvation. The only sign that a Christian has experienced the full grace of God is if salvation has been received; you have been saved through the opening of your eyes and turning from darkness to light; from evil to righteousness. By turning to the light and becoming righteous by the grace of the Holy Spirit, God forgives us of our sins, and we are sanctified by our faith in Christ Jesus. Are you saved, sanctified and filled with the Holy Ghost? Are you leading others to the light and to the Power of God? In your personal Christian experience or in your discipleship, this is the charge. Our job as co-workers of Jesus Christ is to open the eyes of other men and women so that they might develop the ability to discern darkness from light and discern Satan from God. Our job as Christians is to open our eyes and choose the light and the Power of God and receive salvation and sanctification. I believe most Christians have their eyes wide open, but they have not received anything from Christ; they have not received remission of their sins nor salvation. We have to take responsibility for ourselves and for others, understanding that opening our eyes and the eyes of others is only speaking the words concerning the light and the Power of God. It is not salvation; your eyes are only open; you have not received anything. We must not neglect to preach and teach that the speaking of words is not necessarily renewal of the spirit to receive salvation. You have received something, the remission of sins, when you have confessed of your sins; the salvation of your soul, when God's grace sanctifies you in the faith of Christ Jesus. Salvation means you have opened your eyes and are able to receive the forgiveness of sin on the Sovereign Authority of Jesus Christ, Our Lord and Savior, and become saved by the blood of the Lamb.

Salvation is the first work of grace. The second work of grace is sanctification. Sanctification is not something we can request of God; it comes strictly from the grace of God in which the Holy Spirit chooses us for the inheritance of God Almighty. In sanctification the Holy Ghost purposely selects us for the renewal of our spirit, the cleansing of our soul, and the deliberate giving up of our rights to ourselves to Jesus Christ. Sanctification is the forfeiting of our personal interests and becoming rightly connected to Jesus Christ's interest in other men and women—opening the eyes of others. There is no greater calling on the soul: *Open Your Eyes and Receive.*

Week 2 Day 3

THE GREAT TRUTHS OF GOD

"Your eyes saw my unformed body. All the days ordained for me were written in your book before one of them came to be."

—*Psalm 139:16 (NIV)*

It is amazing how we do not allow our natural minds to contemplate as much as they should on the depths of the great and enormous truths of God. There is far more to know concerning this life than we care to think about, or even attempt to get at. *"For you created my inmost being, you knit me together in my mother's womb."* (Verse 13). Do you ever dwell on the inmost being who God created while you were just a fetus in your mother's womb? Do you ever think about the thoughts God put into creating you when your body was still undeveloped; before your fingers and toes were formed; before your heart took its first beat? Psalm 139 proclaims: *"If I go up to heaven, you are there; If I make my bed in the depths, you are there. If I rise on the wings of the dawn, If I settle on the far side of the sea, even there your hand will hold me fast. I praise you because I am fearfully and wonderfully made; your works are wonderful, I know that full well."* Do you recognize that you are fearfully and wonderfully made? Do you know that all of God's works are wonderful? Do you contemplate on these great truths of God? Most of us do not have the prerequisite imagination to go into the depths of human thought where the answers to questions about our ordained life are written. We live these arbitrary lives on the surface of God's truths. We do not think about God on the wings of the early dawn, or about the Lord being the author of the book in which the narratives of our lives were written, even before we had lived one, single day. We lack the imagination to consider the ultimate truths of God.

To fully understand the great and enormous truths of God, we cannot rely simply on conscious human experiences; we need the Holy Spirit to bring to life our subconscious supernatural spirit. If you have become insensitive to or unaware of your human nature, you will use the excuse that you were not conscious of your evil nature toward sin. Reconciling your soul to sin is the very height and depth of the truths of God. Our human nature was created by God when all He had created was our unformed body. Our sinful nature, goodness, thoughts, heart and spirit are all aspects of our innermost being created by God before we were born. Everything you have ever done, and everything you will ever do, has all been preordained by God before you lived even one day. Dwell on that great truth of God.

In relationship with the second coming of Christ, the great truths of God, our inner-most being, our natural human nature, and the cleansing of our sinful soul; *"You hem me in—behind and before; you have laid your hand upon me. Such knowledge is too wonderful for me, too lofty for me to attain. Where can I go from your spirit? Where can I flee from your presence?"* (Verses 5-7). Acknowledging that there are heights and depths in God's great truths that I cannot get to, dreams I will never reach, personal motives I cannot account for, and things that I simply do not understand concerning the Lord, God Almighty; I ask of God, "search me out" and hold my whole spirit, soul and body blameless. *"May God himself, the God of peace, sanctify you through and through. May your whole spirit, soul and body be kept blameless at the coming of our Lord Jesus Christ."* (I Thessalonians 5:23 NIV). You should dwell intensely and for a long while on these things.

THE CONSEQUENCES OF OBEDIENCE TO JESUS CHRIST

*"As they led him away, they seized Simon
from Cyrene, who was on his way in from
the country, and put the cross on him
and made him carry it behind Jesus."*

—*LUKE 23:26 (NIV)*

When we make the decision to obey God, our obedience comes at a cost to us and to others we love and care for. We accept what obedience costs us, but when it costs others, that is where we struggle and become conflicted with our decisions. Because we love Christ Jesus with the wholeness of our heart, obedience is not a burden to us. The burden is on those whom we love, but they do not love Jesus with the same level of intimacy as we do. Carrying the cross behind Jesus may come at no cost to me, but what is the cost to my family, friends and loved ones? Carrying the cross is a delight to me, but a tragedy to my family and others who may be relying on me for their own well-being and self-preservation. More often than not, when I obey Jesus Christ, it runs counter to what others in my life are expecting from me. If I obey Christ and ignore the needs of my spouse, children, parents, friends and acquaintances; there are enormous consequences to me and for them because of my decision. Now, I can make a decision to avoid such consequences; all I need to do is simply not obey Jesus. Simon from Cyrene could have made a decision to remain in Cyrene and not travel in from the country. Instead, he obeyed Jesus and traveled to the place where Jesus was to be crucified. His decision had consequences for him and his family. If we are going to be obedient to God, we must not consider the consequences; we must accept the cost and the consequences; irrespective of who is affected by our decision. It is better to pay the cost of obedience, than to suffer the consequences of disobedience. Those whom you may have interest in saving from the consequences of your decisions cannot save your soul from eternal damnation and give you the gift of sanctification and the Holy Ghost. We must always be willing to choose salvation over everything else.

We have no right to expect anything other than what Jesus Christ experienced. Jesus was crucified, and we should expect to be crucified as well. Carrying the cross of Jesus wanes in comparison to having your side pierced, being nailed to the cross by your feet and hands and having your bones broken creating blood clots; all causing you to suffer excruciating pain while you suffocate under the weight of your own body. Those were the consequences of Jesus being obedient to His Father. We should expect nothing less as the cost of obedience to Jesus. That's why Jesus warned the women who cried out for Him not to, but to cry for themselves. *"Do not weep for me, weep for yourselves and for your children."* (Verse 28.) The warning was there, it is the cost of obedience to Christ Jesus. *"Blessed are the barren women, the wombs that never bore and the breasts that never nursed!"* (Verse 29). There are serious consequences as a result of obedience to Christ; but we must be willing to suffer in the name of Jesus Christ; no matter the cost.

We cannot negotiate the conditions of our obedience, the cost or consequences of our decision to be obedient to God. We can only obey, and what will happen will happen. Simon from Cyrene did not expect to have to bear the cross behind Jesus when he made the decision to obey God and travel to Jerusalem. Where is God sending you? What is God asking you to do? Be obedient, without hesitation or doubt.

Week 2 Day 5

ALONE WITH GOD

"He did not say anything to them without using a parable. But when he was alone with his own disciples, he explained everything."

—MARK 4:34 (NIV)

*O*ur relationship with God is personal. Jesus Christ does not attempt to explain things to us that we are not ready to understand, but when we are ready, Christ takes us up to the mountaintop for some alone time with Him and His Father. Have you ever been alone with God? Jesus speaks to us in parables so that we can understand His teachings. The kingdom of God; "It *is like a mustard seed, which is the smallest seed you plant in the ground. Yet, when planted, it grows and becomes the largest of all garden plants, with such big* *branches that the birds of the air can perch in its shade."* (Verse 31-32). The work of the Lord is slow and deliberate. By using parables, God drives us deeper into our own soul and wider into our own thoughts. This work takes time; it takes our entire lifetime and all of eternity for God to make us into what He has purposed for our lives. While we are made in God's image, the process of aligning our thoughts, heart and spirit with His spirit, is an enormous undertaking that can only occur during the times we are alone with God. When we are with others, God cannot work on our soul; He can only use what He has made us up to this point. Every person is a work in progress and the process will never end. God's work to better us will never be done. Even in His kingdom, the work will continue. The only way we become of use to God is when we allow God to drag us down into the depths of our inmost being and build our character back up in His image, renewing in us a clean spirit.

We do not recognize the evil instinct, jealousy, envy, hatred, pride, prejudice and laziness of our own heart. God does, and He can only remove all the bad in us and replace it with the perfect character of Jesus Christ, when we are alone with Him. Christ Jesus reveals to us our evil nature when we are alone with Him, and then summons God's grace to begin the work through eternity to makes us what He has purposed for our lives. How many of us have developed the courage to go up onto the mountain alone with God and allow Him to reconstruct our thoughts, redesign our heart and renew our spirit?

The last fraction of pride that must go before God can take us up to the mountain is the part of us that believes we know who we are. We don't know ourselves, others, or God. We don't know how we will respond when the great test comes, because we have not spent enough time alone with God, allowing Him to explain everything to us. Conceit and being a "know-it-all" are the greatest hinderances to developing a spiritual life and deep understanding of God. We are so unworthy of God's love, and the very instance we see ourselves from God's point of view, our unworthiness becomes very apparent. We are nobody until God makes us somebody, and He cannot make us somebody until we are willing to see ourselves as worthless. When we acknowledge that we are worthless, we are then ready to be alone with God; we are ready to be made somebody in God's image. God will continue to pull you down into your own decrepit spirit until you beg for some alone time with Him. This is the place where no pride or conceit is left in you. This is the point of spiritual poverty. This is the only place where God can get you alone, with only Him, and begin to work on your spirit. Get to where you can be alone with God and allow Him to make use of you; allow Him to make you somebody.

Week 2 Day 6

ARE YOU QUIET WITH GOD?

*"The Lord your God is with you, he is
mighty to save. He will take great delight
in you, he will quiet you with his love,
he will rejoice over you with singing."*

—*ZEPHANIAH 3:17 (NIV)*

"*When he was alone with his own disciples.*" God first
gets you alone with Him; then He will quiet you
with His love. God gets us alone with Him by conviction,
affliction, temptation and anticipation. God gets us alone
with Him with heartache, brokenness, disappointment, and

illness. God gets us alone with Him on the line of bruised affection, spiritual poverty, severed relationships and even new relationships. God gets us alone with Him, and we become confounded, and cannot utter a single word. That's when we get quiet with God. That's when God has used His mighty love to get us quiet. Affliction, destitution, and broken-heartedness may not feel like love at times, but rest assured, it is love when God cares enough to get your attention, open your eyes and prepares you to receive forgiveness of your sins and sanctification by faith in Christ Jesus. Once we are alone and quiet with God, He then begins to explain everything and expound upon His teachings. Consider how Jesus taught His disciples. The disciples were the ones who always became confounded and silent. The crowd was never perplexed; others always had something to say. Jesus would quiet His disciples with His love, once they were alone, Jesus would expound upon His teachings with them. The disciples were not conceited and proud with Christ; their spirits were quiet, and they constantly asked Him questions, like little children. Jesus constantly answered their questions with parables that gave them a deeper understanding; but the disciples were not able to understand until Christ had breathed on them and gave up the Holy Ghost to them. (*see* John 14:26). Likewise, we will not understand until we have received the Holy Ghost by the grace of God.

God is not going to sow seeds into our souls until He has prepared us to be the soil that is necessary to produce a crop "thirty, sixty or even hundred times what was sown." (*see the Parable of the Sower*, Mark 4:16-29). God intends to be very clear that this is precisely the only line on which He will deal with our souls. He brings us to this line by conviction, affliction, destitution and broken relationships. He brings us to this line with His love. Although we suffer greatly, we cannot begin to understand the pain and sorrow and confusion of our brothers, sisters and friends; even though we are certain that we can. In our ill-gotten conceitedness, we think we understand everything there is about this life, until God breaks us down, slams our face into the ground and gives us a double-portion of what He has given our friends. We then get alone and quiet with God, saying; "Lord! Have mercy on me! I know nothing about what I am doing." God knows how to get our attention; but we must decide if we will get quiet with God and "open our eyes and receive." Until we get quiet, we cannot receive the Holy Ghost. Until we receive the Holy Ghost, we cannot understand the teachings of Christ. The Holy Ghost will unveil enormous regions of our souls filled with conceit, ignorance, self-grandiosity, stubbornness and unworthiness; and this can only be done when we get alone and quiet with Christ Jesus. We may be alone with Jesus right now; but we cannot get beyond our own noisy thoughts, confused hearts, jittery spirits and self-interests long enough to hear God's voice, or to be of value to His service. The Lord our God cannot take delight in us, rejoice over us or save us until we quiet all the noise in our mind, body and soul and allow Him to quiet us with His love. Are you quiet with God?

THE QUIET VOICE OF GOD

*"Then I heard the voice of the Lord saying,
'Whom shall I send? And who will go for
us?' And I said, 'Here am I. Send me!'"*

—*Isaiah 6:8 (NIV)*

Very seldom does God speak to us in a loud, boisterous voice or an ear-shattering thunderous sound. In fact, God seldom speaks directly to any one person when He says; "Whom shall I send?" Anyone under the sound of the quiet voice of God can answer His call. There were numerous people in ear shot of God's quiet voice when He asked whom shall He send, but it was only Isaiah who answered. Isaiah heard God quietly ask, "Who will go for us?" Isaiah was not part of some rare sect who had a special connection to God allowing him to hear what others could not. Isaiah heard God because he confessed his sinfulness and the sinfulness of the nation before God. God then sent an Angel to cleanse Isaiah's soul; then Isaiah was able to hear and understand the quiet voice of God. When God asks, whom shall I send, who will go for us, that is an all-call to everyone, and anyone can answer. The issue becomes who can really understand what God is saying in His quiet voice. God must alter you, and with His grace cleanse you before you can hear His voice; but hearing God is not the same as understanding God. What you hear depends on your connection to God; and what you understand depends on the altered disposition of your spiritual character, in relation to the perfect dispositions of Jesus Christ. Are you rightly related to Christ to hear and properly understand the quiet voice of God? Have you been altered? "Many are called, but a few are chosen." We must prove to God that we are the choice ones; show that if chosen we will respond with; "Here am I. Send me!" The choice ones are the saints who have come into perfect communion with God, through their relationship with the Atonement of Jesus Christ. When you are rightly related to God through Christ Jesus, the Holy Ghost imparts to you the perfect disposition of the character of Christ. Your disposition in God's character is what unclogs your ears, gives you clear 20/20 vision, and cleanses your spirit. Unclogged ears, clear vision and a clean spirit will allow you to hear the quiet voice of God and answer; "Here am I. Send me!"

"Whom shall I send. And who will go for us?" This is not a line of questioning on which God is attempting to single-out a particular individual and garner his or her response. This is God's quiet voice pushing everyone under the sound of His voice to consider, through personal introspection and self-examination, if they are the chosen ones. Isaiah looked at himself, considered his character, examined his soul and concluded that he was the chosen one; and that is why Isaiah responded in the affirmative. Are you the chosen one? God will not compel you to step up and raise your hand; He will make His request known in a very quiet voice. You will only be able to hear Him if you are in His presence, rightly related in character, thought, heart and spirit. You must abandon the notion that God will come to you with the sound of a trumpet and a thunderous explosion of begging and pleading. When Jesus called His twelve disciples, it was a simple quiet gesture; "Come follow me." He did not encourage their responses with promises of glamour, fame or fortune. He simply said in a quiet, calm and stoic disposition; "I will make you fishers of men." Jesus and His disciples did not ride around in a fancy Rolls Royce or Bentley. They did not reside in mansions and travel in private Learjets. All Jesus offered His disciples was a hard walk with Him and the promise of the face of God.

THE NATURE OF GOD'S VOICE

*"Then I heard the voice of the Lord saying,
'Whom shall I send? And who will go for
us?' And I said, 'Here am I. Send me!'"*

—*Isaiah 6:8 (NIV)*

Why did God send Isaiah out to speak to the people of Judah and Jerusalem on His behalf? Why was God unable to speak to the nation of Israel Himself? When we contemplate the voice of God, we oftentimes fail to consider the nature of God's voice. God is the Holy Spirit; therefore, the nature of His voice is of the Holy Spirit. Because of this fact, you can hear God's voice only if His Holy Spirit is in you; otherwise, you are not of the proper nature to hear God's voice. The different parts of nature have their own unique voice; the sea, the mountains, even the call of the wild have their own unique sound, voice, and call, in accordance with their nature. To hear the call of the wild, the nature of the wild must be in you. To hear the call of the sea or the mountain, the call of the sea or mountain must be in you. These great calls can be heard by only a great few because their calls are an expression of the parts of nature from which they come. There is the call of the city. One must be a city dweller and have the nature of the city in them to hear the voice of the city. We can only hear a voice if the nature of that voice is in us. That is precisely why God could not speak directly to the nation He sent Isaiah to speak to. The nation did not have the nature of God in it; therefore, they would not have heard God's call. Isaiah heard God's call because God cleansed Isaiah and imparted His Holy Spirit in Isaiah. God and Isaiah were of the same nature of the Holy Spirit. "I heard the voice of the Lord, saying Whom shall I send?" The voice of the Lord is the expression of the nature of the Holy Spirit, not our human nature. But there are multiple frequencies to the voice of God. The frequency He uses to speak to me is not the same frequency He uses to speak to you and others. I may not recognize God's word when He is calling you; and likewise, you may not recognize God's voice when He is speaking to me. We all have our own assigned frequency, a special and unique connection, with which we hear the voice of God calling us. To hear God's voice, we must protect and maintain the paramount connection and deep relationship between our souls and the nature of God.

The voice of God is not an expression of my nature. The nature of God's voice is not a dubbing of my natural essence; my instincts, affinities, character, and personal interests are never taken into account. God did not care who Isaiah was by nature; He simply sent an Angel to touch Isaiah's tongue with a hot coal from the burning altar. With this act, God cleansed Isaiah of his sinfulness, severely altering the character of Isaiah, giving him the Spirit of the Lord. God put His nature inside Isaiah. I can never consider who I am, what I am made of, what my interests are, if I want God to place His nature inside me. I must ask God to bring me into the right relationship with Him and cleanse my spirit of my sinfulness. I must pray at the altar and ask God, through His loving grace, to alter my character and my nature; then I can hear God's call and respond with; "Here am I. Send me!" To be brought into the nature of the voice of God is to be severely altered in the most spiritually profound manner. This can only be done by the Holy Spirit. Only then can you understand what you hear, perceive what you see, and answer the call of God with a clean heart.

A NEW LIFE
IN CHRIST

*"We were therefore buried with him through
baptism into death in order that, just as Christ
was raised from the dead through the glory
of the Father, we too may live a new life."*

—ROMANS 6:4 (NIV)

We cannot have a new life in Christ until we have become completely dead to sin. Our old self must completely die off; we must die with Christ on His cross; we must be baptized into death before God the Father, through His glory, can raise us up from our spiritual death into a new life in resurrected Christ. What prevents us from giving up our life in death with Christ? Satan, our sinful nature, our evil desires and personal interests all keep us from being buried with Christ. (*see* Mark 4:15-20). When the word of God is planted in us, Satan attacks us; we fall victim to the trials and tribulations brought on by our own sinful nature; we stress from worry, are deceived by money and wealth, and chase our own misguided self-interests in worthless things. Until we ask God to alter our character through communion with the Father, we will never become the "good soil" necessary for the word of God to bear any good fruit in us. To be buried with Christ through baptism into death we must first completely die to sin. We must be completely dead to sin so that Satan cannot destroy the word of God within us. We must die to our own sinful nature so that persecutions do not cause us to deny Jesus in times of trials and tribulations. We must forfeit our rights to ourselves so our own self-interests, worry and money will not destroy our souls. We must die to sin and to ourselves before the word of God can be planted in us and produce 30, 60 or even 100 times what was planted. The old life must be buried in order for God to raise us up in a new life in Christ.

Have you really been buried with Christ? Are you really dead to sin? It can be a tender notion to believe that you have. We have often come to the precipice, the edge, with death, but never gone through with it. We consider the consequences of obedience to God and turn back. We determine that the cost of dying with Christ in baptism comes at too great a price. We don't want to give up our sinful ways; we don't want to disappoint others who depend on us; we want to believe the deceit of money and wealth; we want to pursue our own self-interests and meaningless desires. Dying to sin is very difficult to do, but we must die a spiritual death before we can be buried with Christ in His death. We must be baptized into the life, death, resurrection and ascension of Christ; it is not a death of no longer being. When you are baptized into the death of Christ, God the Father will cleanse your spirit and give you a new life in Christ. You will produce good fruit from the word of God that the Holy Ghost will plant in your soul.

Have you really had your spiritual funeral or are you fooling yourself? Are you really willing to accept the consequences of obedience to the word of God? Will this be your last day on earth as a dead Christian? Will you die with Christ on the cross and allow God to raise you from your spiritual death, giving you a new life in Christ? Will you ignore the Devil, forfeit your rights to yourself, and devote loyalty to Christ? If your answer is yes, then this will be your last day on earth. God will raise you up, just as He raised Jesus Christ up from His earthly tomb. This is God's will. When you realize God's purpose for your life, you will enter into communion with the, Lord God Almighty; and into sanctification through the Atonement of Christ as naturally as taking a breath.

PREPARING YOUR SOUL FOR THE WORD OF GOD

"Others, like seed sown on good soil, hear the word, accept it and produce crop—thirty, sixty or even a hundred times what was sown."

—*MARK 4:20 (NIV)*

Seed fallen along the path. *"As he was scattering his seed, some fell along the path, and the birds came and ate it up."* (Verse 4). Seed fallen along the path is the word of God that has fallen on the deaf ears of evil doers who have found work in the Devil's workshop. These seeds, the word of God, are quickly eaten by the birds. The birds are symbolic of the Devil in this passage. *"As soon as they hear it, Satan comes and takes away the word that was sown in them."* (Verse 15.) For the unbeliever and evil doers, Satan quickly removes the word of God from their thoughts, so the word has no chance of sprouting roots. The path is like a soul that is not properly prepared to receive the word of God. The word of God that has fallen on the wicked, wrongdoers, and demon possessed will bear absolutely no fruit.

Seed sown on rocky places. "Some fell on rocky places, where it did not have much soil. It sprang up quickly, because the soil was shallow." (Verse 5). Seed that has fallen on rocky places is the word of God that has been heard and received with exceeding joy to those who are open to God's teachings; but they still do not know how to live the word; the word to them just sounds good, but they are not quite ready to live in accordance to God's will. The word grows short and thin roots in the soul of the hearer; therefore, the frailness of the word cannot grow into a strong spiritual crop. This is like a babe-in-Christ who has just been introduced to Christ. They quickly abandon the teachings of Jesus Christ as soon as there is drama in their life. They are quick to turn back to their natural dependencies: alcohol, drugs, overeating, gossip, ill-temperament, jealousy or greed. (*see* Verse 17). The word of God that falls onto our basic human instincts, proud-nature, under-developed belief, trust and faith in God, cannot bear good fruit. A person quickly runs from the word of God at the first sign of trouble, if his or her soul is in a rocky place. A place with very little soil, not properly prepared for the planting of the word of God.

Seed sown among thorns and thistle. *"Other seed fell among thorns, which grew up and choked the plants, so they did not bear grain."* (Verse 7). Seed that has fallen among thorns and thistle is the word of God heard by those who are still dealing with worry, deceit from money and wealth, and their own self-interests. (see Verse 19). Worrying, the evils associated with being deceived by money, and personal desire, chokes out the word of God in your life. Relying on money prevents you from trusting in God. Worrying yourself sick destroys your faith in Christ. Your own crooked desires are a hinderance to you living a life of sacrifice unto the Lord. The word of God cannot produce good crop in an environment ruled by money, self-righteousness, envy, deceit, dishonesty, and worry. Beware of anything that contaminates your soul in, and loyalty to, Jesus Christ.

Seed sown on good soil. Good soil is a saint who has reconciled to sin and ignores Satan. You are loyal to Christ and His teachings. You do not abandon the word of God when troubled or persecuted. You stay the course and suffer with Christ. You are not deceived by or rely on money and wealth. Your faith is strong, and you believe in the word of God. You have forfeited the rights to yourself. You are broken bread and poured out wine. The roots of the word of God run deep into your thoughts, heart and spirit.

Week 3 Day 4

PREPARED FOR SERVICE IN CHRIST

*"I did not receive it from any man,
nor was I taught it; rather, I received
it by revelation from Jesus Christ."*

—GALATIANS 1:12 (NIV)

Once the Holy Ghost prepares your soul for the word of God; Christ reveals the service of your natural life, the work God has called you for. You do not receive the revelation of what you are here to do from another person, nor are you taught, concerning your service, through academic study or personal thought. The call of God is in alignment with the nature of God that has been placed within you and the particular line connecting you to the word of God. You are not called to a particular service; but rather, a particular nature of work that you have been prepared for, consistent with what Christ has revealed to you about yourself. In keeping with your natural life, God calls you to the work He has prepared you for; and you serve God by doing what fits your personality and nature. *"But when God, who set me apart from birth and called me by grace..."* (Verse 15). God setting you apart from birth is God giving you a unique nature that is unlike the nature of any other human; and it is by His grace that He makes you who you are; whether you are a scholar, intellectual, statesman, politician, street sweeper, bill collector, or saint; who you are by nature is by God's grace. God could have given you any nature. Who you are is exactly who He meant for you to be; and when He is pleased, He will reveal the service in Christ for which He prepared you. *"But when God was pleased to reveal his Son to me so that I might preach him for among the Gentiles."* (Verse 15). The call of God is an expression of the nature of His voice; and service is the realization of my nature. Like the Apostle Paul, I must realize what God has called me to do by realizing the nature He has given me and recognizing the nature with which God calls me.

When I am at work, I preach the word of God. When I am with my family, I preach the word of God. When I am in the valley of the destitute, I lift up the brokenhearted and the demon possessed. When I am being persecuted in

God's name, I lift up the name of the Lord. I am prepared to produce good crop and serve the Lord. The service in Christ I am prepared for is a reflection of my nature and also an overabundance of my love for Christ and His revelation. I don't need to change who I am to serve the Lord. God will alter me until He is pleased and ready to send me out into the world. God sends me where He will, and I accept the consequences of obedience to Christ. That is the nature of the saint in God's service. I am a witness and an example unto the Lord—that means a service of unsullied, uncompromising, and unbridled devotion to Christ Jesus, an undying and unyielding commitment to His service wherever He sends me. God gets me into a relationship with Himself and His word whereby I hear, accept and understand the nature of His call. I then react with my nature aligned to God's nature out of pure love for pleasing my Lord. Service in Christ for the Father is the purpose-driven, nature-guided, soul-prepared, gift of love that I am fitted for. The voice of God comes with a specific natural call. God places inside me a particular essence. When I hear the quiet sound of His Divine call, my nature and His nature work together to reveal my service in Christ. The Lord, God, Almighty reveals Himself to my nature, and I preach Him everywhere He sends me. I serve Him in the most ordinary ways with my life in devout devotion to the Father, Son, and Holy Ghost.

Week 3 Day 5

WHEN DARKNESS COMES OVER YOU

*"Abram fell into a deep sleep, and a thick
and dreadful darkness came over him."*

—GENESIS 15:12 (NIV)

When darkness overcomes you, God is blocking out the light that distracts you from seeing His vision. It is much easier to focus on what God is trying to get you to see when you are in the midst of dreadful darkness. When God gives you His vision, He is placing you in His hands which provide a shadow of darkness over you. In the darkness of the shadow of God's hands you are to do nothing but be sit still and listen. This darkness has nothing to do with nightfall, but everything to do with God going silent on you. He is trying to get the last of whatever is standing in His way, out of you. When God becomes silent with His blessings and rewards, He is forcing out the last bit of self-interest and self-acknowledgement that prevents you from relying completely on Him. There is also a darkness we bring onto ourselves when we expose ourselves to too much artificial light. Artificial light in this sense is the essence of your own soul which causes you to believe you have enough knowledge and resources to do it yourself. You tell yourself you don't need God; so, you never take anything to God in prayer. You tell yourself; "I got this! I don't need Jesus." But God needs you to see and acknowledge His vision; so, He gives you a "time out." He says, "Go sit down and listen." In Abram's case, Abram fell into a deep sleep, and God went silent on Abram for 13 years. When God gives you a vision and a dreadful darkness falls over you, it is time to sit, be silent, listen and wait on the Lord. God will work out everything in accordance to His will and purpose. Don't make the mistake of believing you can help God; you will only get in His way. In the thirteen years that Abraham waited on God, the Holy Ghost removed all self-interest and self-worth from Abraham. No self-reliance on human instincts or common sense remained in Abraham. Like Abraham, our time of silence is meant to give us the opportunity to develop discipline, devotion and obedience, not a time of despair and doubt.

God says, when we wait on Him in the dreadful darkness; *"Do not be afraid, I am your shield, your very great* believe we are in control of our lives. We believe we engineer our own circumstances. Yeah, we will say God orders our steps, but we really don't believe it. We can't even count the number of hairs on our head. How can we possibly be in control of our circumstances. When we find ourselves in the mist of the many momentary troubles or blessings that God engineers for us, we are quick to give credit or blame to another person, but never God. We will say, "The Devil made me do it" before we utter; "God did this on my behalf, for my own good." The Lord, God, Almighty rains down His blessings upon us and His wrath according to His purpose in our lives. He ends marriages to save souls. He sends terminal illness and physical afflictions so we can achieve an eternal glory. He makes the rich poor and the poor rich to shame us into obedience and to encourage our loyalty.

To have abandoned faith in all circumstances of your life demonstrates that you have a committed loyalty to Jesus Christ. God delivers us from a particular set of circumstances; perhaps it is a broken heart, alcohol addiction or a complex issue with our imperfections, and we believe we got over our troubles on our own. This causes us to miss the good that God intended to bring into our lives. When Jesus walked on the water and calmed the seas for the disciples, He said to the disciples- since they feared for their lives after just being a witness to the miracle of feeding the multitude- that they had missed the good in the meaning of the miracle. We miss the good in the meaning of the many blessings the Holy Ghost delivers because we lack faith and loyalty in Christ. If we have faith and are loyal to Jesus Christ, why would we ever worry in the middle of a storm? Storms in our lives are engineered by God on our behalf; therefore, in the midst of storms God works for the good of those who love Him. But the good is for those who have been called according to His purpose. Things do not work for the good of our interest or the interest of friends, wives or husbands, but according to God's purpose. Jesus did not heal the sick, turn water into wine or bring Lazarus back from the dead, just to comfort the heart of family members, to make wedding goers happy or to bless Lazarus' family. He performed His miracles for His Father's own purpose. In fact, God engineered the circumstances that led to the death of Lazarus just so Christ could raise him from the dead, and God could receive the glory—according to His purpose. God is not a vending machine that dispenses blessings anytime we insert a prayer. We have to learn to worship God, and when we do, He will change our circumstances in two blinks of an eye, the very moment He decides to. We cannot pray ourselves out of our circumstances; but what we can do is worship God in sickness and in health. What we can do is have faith at the midnight hour. What we can do is remain loyal in the worst of times.

Week 6 Day 6

THE MOST EXCELLENT WAY

"And now these three remain: faith, hope and love. But the greatest of these is love."

—*1 Corinthian 13:13 (NIV)*

Jesus teaches us that the most excellent way for saints to love is to love other people in the manner Jesus loves them. We must rightly relate ourselves with the love Christ has for other people, in a manner that does not reflect our version of love or interest in other people. *"For His name's sake they went forth."* (3 John 7). Yes, even in love we must do so in the name of Jesus, and in the perfect disposition of Jesus. We must love Christ, then love others the way Christ loves them. The test of our love for Christ is in our practical interest in loving others the way Jesus loves them. The perfect love of Jesus is absolutely the most excellent way; it is even greater than having faith and hope. *"If I have a faith that can move mountains, but have not love, I am nothing."* (Verse 2). When Christ teaches love, it is not a sentimental feeling, but rather an act that is the manifestation of our love for Him. So, what does the love of Christ look like in practice? *"Love is patient, love is kind. It does not envy, it does not boast, it is not proud. It is not rude, it is not self-seeking, it is not easily angered, it keeps no record of wrongs. Love does not delight in evil but rejoices with the truth. It always protects, it always trusts, always hopes, always perseveres."* (Verses 4-7). The challenge is in the practical, not the sentimental. Like is sentimental. Love is an action that imparts the perfections of Christ, based in the power of Redemption, ordained by the Holy Ghost. When you say you love someone with the love of Christ, is that just a warm and gentle feeling, or is it an act of patience, kindness, politeness, humbleness and calm temperament? Does your love protect, trust, offer hope and perseverance? What does your love actually do? What does it produce? Do you love with the love of Christ, the way He loves you?

My love for Jesus Christ is the supernatural power of Redemption pushed into me by the Holy Spirit; and it causes an undeniable loyalty and love to the Lord that manifests itself in my actions toward everyone I meet. If I truly love Christ; I will be loyal to Him at all times; and fully manifest His love.

"Lovest thou Me?" "Feed My sheep." I identify myself with the love of Christ when I feed His sheep in the manner in which He feeds me. Everything passes away, there is a season for everything, except love. Knowledge decreases, skill goes away, faith wanes, hope diminishes, prophesy ceases, tongues quieten, and sentiment is temporary; but love is forever, and it never fails. *"Love never fails."* (Verse 8). Love is the most excellent way. Loyalty and love toward Christ Jesus is the most excellent way; it never fails. Love is perfect, while all other sentiments are imperfect. All gifts from God are temporary, while love is permanent. As we mature in our loyalty to Christ, the perfections of love push away the imperfections in our natural lives, allowing love to reign supreme to faith and hope. We have nothing if we don't have love. We have nothing if we don't have Christ the Lord. We have nothing if we don't have the power of the Redemption through the Holy Ghost. We must love Jesus with an undeniable love, affection and devotion; attached to nothing and no one, but the love of Christ and Christ Himself. Understand that all we have is faith, hope and love in Christ the Lord, and love is the greatest of the three. *"If I give all I possess to the poor and surrender my body to the flames, but have not love, I gain nothing."* (Verse 3.)

Week 6 Day 7

LET GO AND LET GOD

*"I have been crucified with Christ and I
no longer live, but Christ lives in me."*

—*GALATIANS 2:20 (NIV)*

Christ cannot live in me until I completely let go of the entire manner in which I view my life and the world I live in. The idea of letting go and letting God is not just about God saving me from sin, but rather God saving me from my way of looking at all things. Before I can be saved from my own way of living, I must confess all my wicked ways and be washed in the blood of Jesus—crucified with Christ on the Cross and born-again of the Spirit of God. Then I can let go and let God. Once I let go, God can then take hold of my entire being and place the perfect character of Christ in me. Until God gets all the dirt and contamination out of me, Christ cannot live within me. On the onset, it is not about whether or not God can put His faith, goodness, knowledge, self-control, perseverance, godliness, brotherly-kindness, and love inside me. While He wants to build all these things in me, He first wants me to get rid of all sinfulness, evil desires and wickedness. Then God can plant inside me righteousness and holiness. He can then take hold of me and beat me into the shape of His vision, which is Christ in me. Becoming the shape of the vision can only occur after I have reached a level of spiritual poverty in which I present myself to the Lord worthless and relying completely on Him to take control of my life. I must let go of everything that makes me right, proud and arrogant, before God can take hold and make me His humble child.

There is always more for me to let go of, but I can't get to that point until the Holy Ghost intervenes by way of intercessory prayer and prays for me along the line of God's will and purpose for my life. The intervention of the Holy Ghost cannot occur until I give up the rights to my personal life. I have the right to be guided by my own free-will and self-interests. God will never take away my right to myself. I must willfully volunteer to give up that right. I must be willing to become a living sacrifice and abandon myself and all that I possess to Christ before Christ can live in me. If I cannot let go, God cannot take hold. Letting go means putting nothing or no one before God. I must let go of the people I love the most and the things I treasure the most. God is a selfish God, and nothing can come before Him. *"If you want to be perfect, go sell your possessions and give to the poor, and you will have treasures in heaven. Then come, follow me."* (Matthew 19:21 NIV). Letting go means having no treasures on earth that I value more than being in perfect union with Jesus Christ.

"Selling all of your possessions" is a painful human process; because in the natural life, we are so focused on material possessions. We lie, steal and kill to gain wealth, power and prestige. God says we must give it all up to follow Him. We must not only give it up, we also can no longer have a desire for those things that exist outside of God's will. "Your will, Lord! Not mine!" We must focus on and see ourselves from the perspective of God's interests, not our personal interests. Our own interests can only serve as a conduit of resentment toward God and rebellion against the perfect character of Christ. We must be crucified with Christ and share in the horror and the tragedy of the Cross. Once we go through the trauma caused on the Cross of Christ, God will take hold and make us everything He has purposed our lives for.

Week 7 Day 1

RECONCILED
BY THE CROSS

*"God made him who had no sin to
be sin for us, so that in him we might
become the righteousness of God."*

—2 Corinthians 5:21 (NIV)

"*Therefore, if anyone is in Christ, he is a new creation;
the old has gone, the new has come!*" (Verse 16). What
does it really mean to be a new creation? What is the old
that has gone? What is the new that has come? Because we
are born into sin, sin is the essence of life. Sin is not a covert
act of wrongdoing; it is a sense of wrong "being" according

to Oswald Chambers, *My Utmost for His Highest*. There is no heaven, or hell is an act of wrongdoing; but there is hell in wrong "being." Doing is simply an act; but "being" is of the heart and soul, which expresses your fundamental relationship with Christ. Wrong being is a conscious and very concise separation from the love of and the reliance on God. In Christians, the old that has gone is the nature of sin that causes "wrong being." The new that has come is the heredity of life, being rightly connected to the perfections of Christ and the love of God. You are a new creation when you have reconciled to sin and have received the Redemption of the Holy Ghost. You are a new creature in Christ in perfect communion with the righteousness of God. You are no longer a sinner; though you may commit a sinful act, you are no longer "wrong being." Jesus Christ became sin for us and put us under the Grace of God. When God made Jesus sin, the first thing He had to deal with was our inheritance of sin and the fact that we ignore sin as an inheritance; therefore, weakening the power and the condemnation of the word of God. The teachings of Christ, the Gospel of the Lord, the word of God, comes to life and whips our spirit only after we have become a new creation.

Christ Jesus did not simply take on fleshly sin on our behalf, but rather He dealt with the heredity of sin which cannot be dealt with by anyone of the human race. This is something that could only be done by the Son of Man. We are able to be made a saint only because God made His only begotten Son sin for us, "so that in Him we might become the righteousness of God." Jesus was able to do this because he identified with sin in the exact same manner that we, in the flesh, identify with sin. Jesus was tempted by sin just as we were. Therefore, He fully understood the travesties and the trappings of "wrong being." Because Jesus was made flesh, He knew firsthand why we love darkness. Jesus did not sympathize with us; He empathized with us. He experienced sin just as we do! That is why Christ took the entity of sin amassed by the collective human race upon Himself and died on the Cross, in sin, so that we could be saved. Jesus did not have to die for our sins. Christ became the perfect living sacrifice for man so that we could become the righteousness of God and have eternal life. Jesus put us back under the power of Redemption and recreated, renewed and redesigned the essence of the human race. By His crucifixion, Christ placed the human race back into the eyes of God where God intended Adam and Eve to be. Anyone can enter into perfect communion with God because of what Christ accomplished on the cross. We have been reconciled back to God by the Cross of Jesus Christ.

We cannot redeem ourselves; Redemption can only come from the Holy Spirit being placed in us by Our Lord. God's Redemption is wholly and complete; there is nothing else. Christ has done all the heavy lifting. We simply need to ask God to make a new creature in Christ; and do away with "wrong being."

THE JUDGEMENT SEAT OF CHRIST

"For we must all appear before the judgement seat of Christ, that each one may receive what is due him for the things done while in the body, whether good or bad."

—2 CORINTHIANS 5:10 (NIV)

Christ is not only our Redeemer, Savior, and Lord; He is also the Alpha and the Omega; He is the Way, the Truth, and the Life. And yes! Christ is also the Supreme Judge. The Bible asserts that every man, woman and child who has ever lived "must appear before the judgement seat of Christ."

Going before the judgement seat of Christ is a guarantee for all, saint and sinner alike. *"Now it is God who has made us for this very purpose and has given us the Spirit as a deposit, guaranteeing what is to come."* (Verse 5). The Spiritual deposit of the Holy Ghost, Whom God places inside my soul, guarantees I will go before the judgement seat of Christ. I am made by God for this very purpose. If I learn to walk every second of every minute, and every minute of every hour, and every hour of every day, in the light of the glory of the Kingdom of God, then I will, in great delight, look forward to going before the judgement seat of Christ. On the other hand, If I fail to deny myself, insist on walking in the darkness of my own selfish interests, never abandoning myself to Christ, then I will, in grave fear, shudder at the thought of going before the judgement of Christ. *"We are confident, I say, and would prefer to be away from the body and at home with the Lord."* (Verse 8). Whether we look forward to the judgement seat of Christ or shudder in fear of it all, depends on what we do while in the body. It is best that we forfeit the rights to our bodies and live in the light of the words of Christ Jesus; for we will be judged for every deed we do while in the fleshly body.

We must keep ourselves at home with the Lord, praying constantly, giving thanks always, delighting in the deposit of the Spirit, walking upright in the most righteous and holy manner possible. A wrongful thought, a bad temper, an evil desire, a sinful deed will all lead to suffering under the judgement seat of Christ. Going before the judgement seat of Christ is not some end-of-life high-stakes summons where you are read a long laundry list of things you did while you were living. While there is judgement at life's end, handed down by God, Almighty, the judgement of Christ occurs daily while we are living in the fleshly body. Christ judges your bodily deeds immediately. Because Christ died on the Cross to save us from sin, we are judged, convicted and instantly held responsible for our sins. Likewise, when we do good things at home with Christ, we are instantly judged and blessed according to the purpose of God. We are saved, sanctified and filled with the Holy Spirit by the Redemptive Power of the Cross; and we are subjected to the judgement seat of Christ at any moment while in the natural body. When you sin, snatch it immediately into the light of the Redemption and confess your guilt before the Lord Jesus. Throw yourself upon the mercy and goodness of the court of Christ. "Lord! Please have mercy!" If you don't, Christ will immediately convict you of your sin, and God will hand down the punishment. The punishment for sin is self-condemnation in sin. God punishes you, then you punish yourself in double measure. There are some sins we commit that no amount of praying, no length of fasting, no degree of sacrificing, no manner of struggle nor strife will ever stop. There are some sins we commit for so long that we don't recognize them as a sin any longer. Only the Holy Ghost can intervene on our behalf in the case of sins that have become inherent iniquities to who we are in our natural body.

Week 7 Day 3

DESIRES OF
THE HEART

*"For where your treasure is, there
your heart will be also."*

—MATTHEW 6:21 (NIV)

The heart desires what the soul treasures. If your soul treasures earthly things, your heart will desire earthly things as well. Likewise, if your soul treasures heavenly things, then your heart will desire things that are from God in Heaven. We cannot serve two masters— one on earth and one in heaven. "No one can serve two masters." Either you desire sin or you desire righteousness. You are either a slave to sin or a slave to righteousness. You love one and despise the other. *"Don't you know that when you offer yourselves to someone to obey him as slaves, you are slaves to the one whom you obey—whether you are slaves to sin, which leads to death, or slaves to obedience, which leads to righteousness."* (Romans 6:16 NIV). What the heart desires is the key to the Kingdom of God. If you desire righteousness in all regions of your heart, then you will become a slave to Obedience, "which leads to righteousness." Therefore, you must guard your heart and not allow the desires of your heart to become corrupted by sin. If you allow your heart to be corrupted by sin, then you will be a slave to sin, "which leads to death."

The first thing you must do in examining the desires of the heart that enslaves you, is to accept the fact that your sinful thoughts are the reason you are a slave to sin. You are responsible for holding your thoughts captive to enslave yourself to obedience. If you cannot control your evil, sinful, selfish, jealous, greedy, envious thoughts, you will cause your heart to become corrupt, and you will be a slave to sin. But, if you develop the discipline to hold your natural thoughts captive and develop the critical desire for righteousness, then you will become a slave to obedience, "which leads to righteousness." You are the one responsible for the desires of your heart. If you desire to follow your own self-interests, then you will be a slave to yourself. But, if you desire to follow Jesus, then you will be a slave to Christ Jesus. If you love God, you will despise yourself. If you love yourself more than you love God, you will resent God. "You cannot serve two masters."

You cannot serve sin and righteousness; you must choose in your heart which you will be a slave to. We cannot free ourselves from sin, nor can we ask God for righteousness. The Holy Ghost is the guard over sin and gatekeeper to righteousness. But we are responsible for the desires of our heart.

There is absolutely no power on earth capable of breaking the hold of natural desires and delivering us from sin; that power is found only in the Redemption and the power of the Holy Ghost to intervene on our behalf. Where we do have control is in what we decide to give-in to. When we give-in to lust, greed, hatred and sexual immorality, we are a slave to such things. Once we have become enslaved, only the Holy Ghost can break the chains. We are completely powerless in breaking the chains of our own self-imposed enslavement. There is no amount of praying that can be sent up from earth to save us, only the prayer of the Holy Ghost has that power. The desire of our heart must align with the will of God, and that alignment is only along the line of righteousness; not blessings and not deliverance—but only righteousness. So, if you desire the power of the Holy Ghost to intervene in your circumstances, then you need to get the desires of your heart aligned to the Righteousness of God. Become a slave to obedience and let your heart desire only the treasures in heaven.

Week 7 Day 4

MORE THAN A CONQUEROR

"No, in all these things we are more than conquerors through him who loved us."

—*ROMANS 8:37 (NIV)*

In the natural human existence, everything we encounter from life's beginning to life's end is designed to create a separation between us and the love of God. But Paul
reminds the saint that; *"neither death nor life, neither angels
nor demons, nor the present nor the future, nor any powers,
neither height nor depth, nor anything else in all creation, will
be able to separate us from the love of God."* (Verses 38 &

39). The life of the saint is lived on a metaphorical spiritual square, and all of life is designed to knock saints off their square. If the devil can get you off your square, he believes he can drive a wedge between the saint and the love of God that is in Jesus Christ, our Lord. But irrespective of the endless efforts of the devil and any power on earth, nothing can cause a separation between saints and the love of God. Nothing can drive a wedge between us and the love of God, we are much more than conquerors through Jesus Christ. While there are many worldly things capable of coming between God and our daily spiritual practices, our prayer life and our religious rituals, these things do not have the ability to alter God's love for us. The cornerstone of Christianity is the love of God that can never be removed from the foundation upon which our relationship with God is built. This foundation is unshakable; not even the earthquakes and stormy circumstances of life can shake the foundation of the relationship we have with God. While we are unworthy of God's love, and while there is nothing we can do to deserve His love, God will never deny us His love. For this reason, Paul says we can stare into the eye of the greatest storm and know that we are more than conquerors through God who loves us. Through heartache and sickness, we are more than conquerors. Through jealousy and hatred, we are more than conquerors. Through destitution and devastation, we are more than conquerors. No matter the circumstance, we can come through smelling like saints through him who loved us.

The most overwhelming of life circumstances, the most extraordinary strain possible on the spirit, and the greatest struggles possible in nature produces the opportunity for the saint to show the world just how great God is. The saint welcomes the most challenging conditions because the saint knows that the love of God is the greatest when the challenge is the toughest. Have you ever seen the love of God shine light in places where you had no idea light could ever shine? That is the love of God. Have you ever had your ship make it to shore when you were certain it would not make it through the storm? The love between God and the saint is inseparable. When you understand that through the love of God we are more than conquerors, the trials, tribulations, setbacks, breakups, and storms are the very things in life that create moments of exceeding joy in the saint. Paul says, "I am exceedingly joyful in all our tribulations." If you are not standing on top of your circumstances like a master surfer standing on his surfboard and riding the wave of life, then you do not believe in the love of God. The saint knows that the love of God cannot be altered. Therefore, she walks around with an unshakable confidence in knowing that, irrespective of circumstance, the love of God, which is in Christ Jesus, is not going to allow the things of this world to knock her off her square.

Week 7 Day 5

ENDURE UNTIL YOU PERSEVERE

*"Therefore, since we are surrounded by such
a great cloud of witnesses, let us throw off
everything that hinders and the sin that
so easily entangles, and let us run with
perseverance the race marked out for us."*

—*Hebrews 12:1 (NIV)*

There are three basic natural conditions in the life of a saint: your life is either facing a major obstacle, overcoming a major obstacle, or moving towards a major obstacle. Obstacles are a fact of life and there is no point in praying for an obstacle-free existence. There will be obstacles and afflictions along the race that are designed to knock you off your square. God's love and the sufficiency of His grace provide the necessary strength and endurance to persevere in the midst of the most challenging situation. When we believe our situations are hopeless and dire, God says; "throw off everything that hinders" you from believing in Him; and "throw off the sin that so easily entangles" you in a snare of doubt, deceit and destitution. *"I have told you these things, so that in me you may have peace. In this world you will have trouble. But take heart! I have overcome the world."* (John 16:33) Every obstacle you will ever face in life has already been overcome by God and He has given us the victory; we just have to endure with perseverance. God's desire is that saints lack nothing as we run the race marked out for us. *"Perseverance must finish its work so that you may be mature and complete, not lacking anything."* (James 1:4) We must finish the race. I recall an Olympic track and field event where a runner became injured in the middle of the race. He fell down in agony, picked himself up off the track, and limped around the track in tears and dilapidating pain, until he crossed the finished line. Fighting through pain, disappointment, adversity and affliction to finish the work brings about a level of maturity and completeness that can be gained in no other manner. While the Olympian who limped across the finish line finished in last place, he was lacking nothing because his perseverance finished its work. In the race of life we may experience divorce, loss of life, disappointment and major obstacles, like disease and addictions along the way. But we must finish the race.

When we endure joyfully, patiently and faithfully, perseverance finishes its work, and we are victorious in the Lord, God, Almighty! *"Be joyful in hope, patient in afflictions, faithful in prayer."* (Romans 12:12 NIV). If we endure faithfully and righteously to the end, we will receive the inheritance of the promises of the Kingdom of God and all its glory. Life is no fairytale story. It comes with its ups and downs. Defeat and setbacks visit everyone. Heartache will know you by your first name, and pain and suffering will know your last name. With endurance and perseverance, and the love of God, we demonstrate to the great cloud of witnesses that we are more than conquerors in God through our relationship with Jesus Christ, our Lord, and that our God, the Supreme Authority over the race we run, is a good, merciful and faithful God. So that perseverance can finish its work in your life, throw off any and everything that hinders you from crossing the finish line- joyfully, patiently and faithfully. Pray that the Holy Ghost frees you from sin so there is nothing but righteousness along your path. And to all saints; *"Let us fix our eyes on Jesus, the author and perfecter of our faith, who for the joy set before him endured the cross, scorning its shame, and sat down at the right hand of the throne of God. Consider him who endured such opposition from sinful men, so that you will not grow weary and lose heart."* (Hebrews 12:2-3)

GOD'S DISCIPLINE AND HIS PUNISHMENT

"In your struggle against sin, you have not yet resisted to the point of shedding your blood."

—*Hebrews 12:4 (NIV)*

There is bloodshed on the battlefield of Christ. Our Lord and Savior, Jesus Christ, rode into Jerusalem on the back of a donkey to be nailed to a cross, crucified, killed and buried for our sins. Yet, we do very little to resist sin ourselves. We live our lives in expectation and pray to God that we leave the battlefield intact, unscathed, unbruised and without shedding blood. Christ shed His blood for our sins, but we do not risk the shedding of our own blood for our own sins, despite being sons of the Father, Who sent His only begotten Son into the world to save the world. Because we are sons of God and because we have not yet resisted sin to the point of our own bloodshed, God disciplines and punishes us. *"Because the Lord disciplines those he loves, and he punishes everyone he accepts as a son."* (Verse 6). As parents, we discipline our children because we love them and want them to grow up to be well-mannered and well-meaning, productive adults who fear, believe in, worship and love the Lord. We punish them to make them respect the rules we have established. Our goal is to raise our children into maturity and completeness. As children of God, He disciplines and punishes us for the same reasons. God does not spare the rod, as we should not spare the rod with our own children. Discipline and punishment are indications of God's love. *"Endure hardship as discipline; God is treating you as sons. For what son is not disciplined by his father?"* (Verse 7). Enduring hardship is a test of our faith, which develops the strength to persevere under any circumstance. As a father, we want to make sure our children are prepared to go out into the world with the ability to persevere under any circumstance. God desires the same for His children. He prepares us to persevere in the race He has purposed us for. The race is always against sin, and we must resist sin to the point of bloodshed. We must be willing to give our lives, be broken bread and poured out wine, for righteousness' sake. Many of us are not even able to deny ourselves and our personal interests to follow Jesus or live a life of sacrifice in

Christ, much less resist in the struggle against sin. God's discipline and His punishment are intended to help us develop the ability to resist sin and throw off everything that hinders us from having a relationship with Him.

"If you are not disciplined (and everyone undergoes discipline) then you are illegitimate children and not true sons." (Verse 8). The true test of whether you are children of God is whether God disciplines you. His discipline demonstrates that you are His legitimate child. In every heartache, in every pain, and in all the struggles through our love for Christ, God is disciplining us so that we may partake in the glory of His righteousness and share in the benefits of His holiness and goodness. God's goodness, mercy, blessings, love, faithfulness and promises are only for His children. There is a reservoir of righteousness, love, peace and mercy that God creates only for His children that is accessed through Christ living in us and it's made available by the tragic bloodshed on the Cross. So, when you find yourself in unfavorable circumstances of hopelessness and despair, when your spouse has left you, when illness is ravishing your body, when you have lost everything of value, remember the story of Job, reconcile to sin, and realize that you are also a child of the Living God. While God dishes out His discipline and punishment in healthy portions, His gifts of righteousness and holiness are extremely rewarding to those trained up in His word. In Christ Jesus, be willing to struggle against sin to the point of bloodshed—your blood and the Blood of Christ.

Week 7 Day 7

LEAVE YOUR
DISCOMFORT

"Get up and take care of your mat."

—*ACTS 9:35*

In Lydda, Peter found a man named Aeneas, who had been bedridden for eight years. After praying over Aeneas and informing him that Jesus had healed him, Peter told Aeneas to; "Get up and take care of your mat." Far too often, we are comfortable in our circumstances—in sickness and health, in sorrow and joy, even though we are not exactly where God wants us to be. God calls saints from the lowest of places, from bedridden illnesses and hopelessness, and instructs—to

Get up and take care of your mat. When God tells us to "get up and take care of your mat," what He is really saying is; "Leave your discomfort."

God calls you to leave your discomfort as well as your comfort because He has a greater work for you to do in accordance to what He has purposed your life for. Sometimes to do things God wants you to do, you must be willing to get up from your discomfort, take up your mat of inconvenience and travel into the wilderness of uncertainty to find your comfort. Many saints use their discomfort as an excuse for not finishing the race. We sit down on God for years, blaming our afflictions. God has overcome all our afflictions. You may not know why God is calling you out of discomfort to take care of your mat; but you must be obedient and get up and take care of everything you have been neglecting. God has a vision, but He does not always reveal it. We walk by faith, not by sight. We must abandon the seen and seek the unseen. Not everything God does in our lives is explainable. There is nothing wonderous, miraculous or amazing about the things that can be explained naturally. Who can explain the miracle of Peter, through Christ Jesus, raising the dead woman, Tabitha, from the dead? But it is also not natural for humans to obey God when He says, "Get up and go"—when He says; "Leave your discomfort." But Tabitha obeyed Peter and sat up after opening her eyes and seeing him. God gives us free will to do whatever we want to do. We even have the option to ignore and disobey God. Tabitha did not have to sit up. Aeneas did not have to get up and take care of his mat.

Obedience is given meaning only when it is done out of the recognition of and devotion to the will of God. It was God's will that Aeneas could walk again, and that Tabitha had life again; they were being obedient to the Supreme Authority of the Holy Spirit, when they obeyed the command to; "Get up" and leave your discomfort. In your daily walk with Christ, are you obedient to the higher authority of God, when He commands you to; "Leave your discomfort?" How do you respond to God's command to; "Get up and go?" Are you still in situations at work, in relationships, within organizations in which God has clearly told you to leave your discomfort and get comfortable being obedient? If you find yourself drowning in unfavorable circumstances, you may want to examine whether or not you are being obedient or disobedient to the commands of the Supreme Authority over your life.

If your boss at work incentivizes your actions by saying to you; "You better get up and do," or "You must do, or else," he fractures the human spirit and potentially causes you to obey out of fear of being fired. This sort of action results from an unclean spirit and does not conform to the teaching of Jesus Christ. You become a slave to your spouse, boss, or organizational leader, unless behind your obedience is a devoted obedience to following Christ and a righteous thirst for God Himself.

Week 8 Day 1

IN THE MIDNIGHT HOUR

"About midnight Paul and Silas were praying and singing hymns to God."

—ACTS 16:25

It is in the midnight hour of struggles, of sickness and of afflictions when God and the Holy Ghost show up in the middle of the prayers and praises of the saints and shakes the foundation of everything that is holding them captive. No matter your circumstance, no power can form against you, for in the midnight hour God is going to show up and turn it around, work it out, and loosen it up. The Holy Ghost lives in the midst of your prayers, and the love of God resides in your praises. The Power in the Midnight Hour is in your belief in the Redemption—the Blood of Jesus Christ paid in ransom for your sin. When you call on the name of Jesus in prayer and in praise of God the Father, in the midnight hour of your divorce, despair or destitution, it is in that very moment you find yourself alone with God. Every other power and dominion over your life has fallen away. So, in the midnight hour, there is no one but you, Jesus and all the other saints. You are there alone; there is nothing around to interfere with your prayer and your praise. Praise Him! It is in the midnight hour that you find yourself on your knees acknowledging to God that you are nothing without Him. It is in the midnight hour that you find yourself in such spiritual poverty that all you can do is call on God; and He shows up, but He shows up with the full Power of the Trinity and steps into the midst of your prayer and praise and causes everything around you to crumble. When you are alone with God, in the midnight hour, the naysayers have gone to sleep; the unbelievers have disbanded and gone home, and those who wish you harm have grown weary. Because the Power of God watches over all saints, we are blessed in and every circumstance, every moment of every day. We are blessed in the valley. We are blessed on the mountaintop. We are blessed in sorrow. We are blessed in pain. We are blessed in the streets, and we are blessed in our afflictions. No power or principality has dominion over the soul of the saint. In the midnight hour God is going to show up and show out in your favor. He is going to cause every spirit that has formed against you to loosen their grip; all of your enemies will flee or be destroyed, and your captors will kneel before you—the devil will be defeated, and God will make Satan wash your feet. That's how powerful our God is!

We serve the true and only righteous God! He raised His Son from a rocky tomb and placed all Power in His Hands. Because of Christ Jesus we will triumph over disease, jealousy, discrimination, hatred and death. Like Paul and Silas, nothing can hold us captive from doing the will of God. "I have never seen the righteous forsaken." Everything works in the favor of those who love the Lord. Don't worry! Late in the midnight hour God is going to show up and turn your whole life around. Christ Jesus is going to work out everything in your favor; the Holy Ghost is going to intervene on your behalf and bless you beyond your dreams, above your hopes and prayers. Try God! When you find yourself in your darkest moment, that is your midnight hour. Your friends have deserted you; your heart is broken; death is all around you and you are surrounded by evil spirits, cheering for your defeat. Drop to your knees and call on the Lord, God, Almighty. Then watch God, the Father, Son and Holy Ghost, step powerfully right into the middle of your prayer. He will snatch you to your feet, place you at the table of those who were investing in your demise, and make them wash your wounds. The light of God is the brightest in the midnight hour. Wait on Him!

HOLINESS IS THE ONLY WAY

*"Make every effort to live in peace
with all men and to be holy; without
holiness no one will see the Lord."*

—*Hebrews 12:14*

W"*orship God acceptably with reverence and awe.*" (Verse 28). We must glorify the Lord in both adoration and fear, and we must live a life of righteousness and holiness. Holiness is the only way to the Kingdom of God. As my creator, I realize that God has a claim on my life, and I have a claim on His many promises, but I cannot get to

His promises without worshipping Him in fear, reverence and awe. How does this manifest itself in reality and spiritually? We worship the Lord with our bodies, and our bodies must be offered to God as His places of worship—Temples for God. Have you made your body a temple for the Holy Ghost? A body that is holy and righteous will always reflect the Light of God upon it, but a body that is not in fear of God will not have the reflection of the Light of God upon it. Does your body reflect the Light of God or is it consumed in darkness? Are you living in peace with all of God's people, or are you consumed by a sinful nature rotted with wrongdoing, sexual immorality and acts against God? When we worship the Lord in reverence and awe, with our bodies as the temple of the Holy Ghost, we do not give our bodies immorally over to sexual desires, physical degradation or wickedness. If we intend to claim the promises of the Kingdom of God, holiness is the only way. In the Redemption, I am given the life of sanctification by the filling of my soul by the Holy Ghost. The Holy Ghost gives me a life of Christ in me, and me in Christ; this is sanctification. Then I must do the work to transform my Holy Ghost filled life into a life of spiritual obedience to God, in holiness and righteousness. The work of transforming my life into a life of holiness is mine to do. It is my responsibility to keep my soul cleansed and my body as a temple of the Lord. God gives us the knowledge, down to the details of His promises, but we must act upon His knowledge and be completely consumed in a life of holiness.

"For our God is a consuming fire." (Verse 29). I must cleanse my body-temple from all contamination, filth and

grime of this world. I must cleanse both my spirit and my physical temple, my natural body, with the consuming fire of God. His consuming fire will burn everything that is not right in my heart, a detriment to my soul, or a hinderance to the claim of God's promises. I am either consumed by the fire of God and my body reflects His flames, or I am consumed in darkness. I can serve only one master. I must put God first in every aspect of my existence and leave everything else alone, or I risk hell. I must fearfully obey unto righteousness and holiness in my every day walk with the Lord. I must be Christ-like in my spirit, forfeiting my right to myself as Christ did. I must constantly, every moment of every day, submit to the will of God, giving no consideration to my own interests or conferring with the opinion or desires of the flesh. It is wholly my responsibility to keep my temple clean and inviting to the Holy Spirit. I must keep my Master's House clean, holy and righteous. If I do my part, the Holy Ghost will surely bring me up to the spiritual realm of God, the Father, and perfect my holiness in the fear of God, so that God will always have His way with my life—His Temple. Let God consume you with His Fire, and let your body reflect the Light of the Lord upon it. Holiness is the only way!

Week 8 Day 3

TAKE UP YOUR CROSS

"If anyone would come after me, he must deny himself and take up his cross and follow me."

—*Matthew 16:24*

Within the verses of *Matthew 16:21-28*, the most powerful message from the Savior in the whole Bible is given to all who wish to see the Kingdom of God—*Deny yourself, take up your cross and follow Jesus!* When I consider my relationship with God, there is no doubt in my natural mind that I have a cross to bear, because I know, unequivocally, that I do; but there is still a question as to if I will actually bear my cross. When I give even greater practical consideration to the righteous words and spiritual commands of God, I acknowledge that I have a race to run in bearing my cross, which first requires me to deny myself the right to my life and my personal interests. I know I must complete the race that God has put before me, and the race is to determine just how quickly and completely I can lose myself in the Redemption of Christ. I cannot be saved until I am willing to lose myself; and I cannot lose myself until I am willing to deny myself. My salvation is wholly dependent upon my self-denial. If I never develop the discipline to deny myself, then bearing my cross for Christ is only a tender notion; for my cross is the same cross Christ Jesus had to bear. Oh, we tell ourselves we are willing to bear our cross. Then we learn what bearing our cross really means; and, suddenly, we turn back.

Jesus died so that I could live. Now, I must die a similar death in the name of Jesus, so Jesus can live in me and through me. I must give my life up for Christ so that I can live in Christ, and He in me. *"For whoever wants to save his life will lose it, but whoever loses his life for me will find it."* (Verse 25). It's not at all about me! It's all about Jesus! It's not about my spouse! It's about Jesus! It's not about my friends, my children or my job, any other human or any particular thing! It's about Jesus! Christ's life was not about Him; It was about His Father. Jesus knew He had to go to Jerusalem to suffer and be killed. Jesus Christ could have chosen not to go to Jerusalem; He could have escaped the soldiers. He could have chosen the life of a rich aristocrat in a distant land or a life of obscurity out of harm's way; but Jesus denied Himself, took up His Cross and followed the will of His Father. How many times have you chosen not to follow Jesus because the cross was too much to bear? Jesus died for all nations. I simply need to die for myself, not the whole world; but I have not proven to be willing to bear that cross. My cross does not remotely bear the weight of the Cross Jesus had to take up. My cross is that God demands I must die spiritually to everything and everyone in my life that is not Godly. The people in my life and the things I have convinced myself I cannot live without; that are not of God, will cause me to rebuke the word of God, instead of rebuking the devil and my sinful desires. When Peter pulled Jesus aside and attempted to rebuke Jesus for saying He must go to Jerusalem to suffer and be killed, Jesus responded, *"Get behind me, Satan! You are a stumbling block to me; you do not have in mind the things of God, but things of men."* (Verse 23). People we love may have good intentions, but the devil will use them to get us to rebuke the word of God. Our friends may not want us to follow Jesus, if following Jesus means we must get away from them. In their selfishness, our friends, family and loved-ones can become "stumbling blocks." Our personal interests become our "stumbling blocks." Self-denial is the starting line of the race God has put before you; and you must run and finish the race with your cross on your back.

Week 8 Day 4

THE ONCE MORE OF GOD

*"Once more I will shake not only
the earth but also the heavens."*

—*Hebrews 12:26*

"*T*he words *"once more"* indicate the removal of what can be shaken.*" (Verse 27). The Lord, God, Almighty has the power to show us things that make us tremble in fear. When God showed Moses the image of the mountain on fire and he heard the words: "If even an animal touches the mountain, it must be stoned," Moses said, "I am trembling with fear." God caused Moses to tremble in fear, and

He causes all saints to tremble in fear; likewise, because He intends to remove something from our spirit. God made us in His image. In our walk, we take upon ourselves things that are not of God, that are not of His image. These things that we create out of our own free-will are shakable—removable, and the fear of God brings about the level of trembling in the soul of man that cause these ungodly, removable things to fall away. When is the last time God caused you to tremble in fear? What did He shake loose? This shaking occurs throughout our lives because God desires that we all become His righteous and holy children. God desires that everyone see the Kingdom of the Most Holy. But He also knows there will be unbelievers, and there will be believers who refuse Him. The Battle of Armageddon at the coming judgement of Christ is where God will destroy the works of Satan "once more." In the Battle of Armageddon, all things born of evil will be shaken, and all things born of the Kingdom of Christ will remain forever. *"So that what cannot be shaken may remain."* (Verse 27). When God causes us to tremble in fear, there is a depth of our spirit that Satan cannot get to. That part of our spirit remains because it is unshakable. The parts of our spirits that are shakable are the parts that we have created, against the will of God. Those are the things of our natural life that are not of God. We create hatred, jealousy, drug addiction, anger and bitterness. God says none of these things will see the Kingdom of Christ, and He shakes them from the spirit of the saint. Divorce, that's God shaking your spirit. Terminal illness, that's God shaking your spirit. Friends fall off, that's God shaking your spirit.

"See to it that you do not refuse him who speaks." (Verse 25). Do not refuse the "once more" of God. This is a stark warning from God. Jesus warned us when He was on earth, and God warns us from Heaven. We have not escaped the warnings of Jesus. The pain and suffering we endure on earth is due to our refusal to obey Christ. In life, we are brutally punished on earth and experience excruciating pain at the temptations of the Devil. If we cannot escape punishment, pain and suffering on earth, we should have no expectation that we will be able to escape the wrath of God that He will shower down from Heaven. There is a huge price to pay for refusing God. *"For our God is a consuming fire."* (Verse 29). The "Once More" of God will be the shaking of both the heavens and the earth. No one will escape the wrath of God. Everything that is shakable will be removed, so there will be only saints who inherit the Kingdom and the glory of God. "Blessed are the meek, for they will inherit the earth." "Blessed are the pure in heart, for they will see God." The Once More of God is the cleansing process that delivers you acceptable in God's eyes and removes all the filth of this life, so that we can join in the procession of saints on the judgement day of Christ, marching into the Light of the Kingdom.

Week 8 Day 5

PLEASING GOD IS THE GOAL

"So we make it our goal to please him, whether we are at home in the body or away from it."

—*2 Corinthians 5:9*

Make it your goal to *please* Him...The goal to please God must be a daily goal, irrespective of your circumstances. Whether you are in the spirit with the body of Christ or in the midst of your human personality, you should be impassioned with the goal to please God in everything you do. The goal for the saint is to be a workman approved by God. *"Do your best to present yourself to God as one approved."*

(2 Timothy 2:15). Everyday, my absolute best for my King; that is the goal. But what exactly does that mean? It means you must hold yourself accountable to God's highest standards in character in every moment of every day. While a workman is tasked with bringing souls to God, spreading the gospel to all nations, and being a witness unto the Lord, your greatest passion has to be "presenting yourself to God as one approved." This is the work of the saint. There should be no greater ambition before you. God does not establish spiritual growth as the goal; but rather pleasing Him as the only goal. Not pleasing God is what leads to spiritual leakage and eventually spiritual failure. Take a daily inventory of the standards you are inspired to meet and ask yourself if those standards are high enough to please God. In this life, we must assume the station of an artist, and our lives are the masterpieces we wish to present to the Lord. In creating ourselves as a masterpiece that we will offer to God, Almighty, we must ensure that what we create within our heart is something that will be pleasing to God. If our heart is holy and righteous and passionately desires to please God, then the masterpiece we create will please God.

Any piece of art that I create, no matter how great others may think it is, that is not created for the sole purpose of pleasing God and meeting His highest standards, will not present me before God as approved. I cannot veer away from the goal of pleasing God, not even in the slightest manner. If I do, I risk my inheritance of the treasures of the Kingdom of God. We must understand at all times where our actions will take us. While there may not be heaven or hell in a particular sinful act, the act may very well lead you in the direction of either heaven or hell. You want to make sure your actions will always lead you to heaven. This is why it is necessary to live in accordance with the perfect standards of Christ, in character and in worship. The daily comparison of your character to Christ's standards is the litmus test for whether you are meeting the goal of pleasing God. *"I beat my body and make it my slave so that after I have preached to others, I myself will not be disqualified for the prize."* (1 Corinthians 9:27).

I must discipline myself to subjugate everything I do and everything I think, to the highest standards of Christ. I must do this incessantly every moment of every day, if I intend to please God and present myself to Him as one approved. God's pleasure in me, in the body of Christ, is determined by the standards I maintain when I am away from Him. Do I aim to please God in all aspects of my being and prove myself to be acceptable to Him every day, or do I have some other motive, irrespective of how noble a motive it might be? The life of the saint is not about being a good person who does many great and noble things. Hell will be filled with many great and noble men. The life of the saint is all about pleasing God.

BY FAITH YOU ARE TESTED

*"By faith Abraham, when God tested
him, offered Isaac as a sacrifice."*

—*Hebrews 11:17*

B y faith we believe God created the heavens and the earth. By faith Noah built the Ark. By faith we believe in the Holy Trinity of God. By faith Abraham obeyed God. Living by faith creates a personal relationship with God and also creates a separation from others in our lives. No one else would have built the Ark. No one else would have sacrificed his only son. Noah and Abraham having lived by faith are examples of how faith separates us from others. By faith Abraham took his family to another land and separated himself from everyone he previously knew. In these modern times we are seldom asked by God to live the kind of faith demonstrated by Noah and Abraham; no one is building arks or sacrificing their first born. Today the test of faith is more about testing our mental and moral separation from the people, places and things we cherish the most. Oftentimes, God gives us a totally different belief on matters and tests us to see if we are willing to walk alone by faith in a belief that no one else we know espouses to. By faith we are called to walk alone emotionally and pragmatically, and separate from those we love, those who do not have a personal relationship with the Lord. This is the message in the Parable of the Great Banquet in Luke, chapter 14. By faith we are all planning a great banquet, only to find out that the guests we intend to invite are not the ones God intends for us to invite. We learn that God has another purpose for our banquet, as our friends and others we know decline the invitation. By faith you can plan your great banquet, but God controls the guest list.

Faith never knows who is on the guest list. Faith never knows what will wash up on the shore; only God knows. By faith we don't care where we are being led or who we will encounter. All we are concerned with is being obedient to God. Noah did not care about the guest list for the Ark. Abraham did not care about the land God directed him to go to; they both built and traveled, respectively, by faith. The key to living by faith is having no personal interest in the outcome; just an interest in the One Who directs you to "do" and "go." The biggest obstacle to faith is expecting a return on your investment, on your terms. God says spread the gospel to all nations, who gets saved is not our decision to make.

The purpose of living by faith is the development of the perfect character of Christ. First, we are separated from others, then we learn we can have no interest in the outcome; and, finally, we attain the character of the Lord. The attainment of perfect character takes on many different looks during the transfiguration of the saint. Initially, faith is temporary, as in the feeling that overcomes us in times of prayer and worship. But we return to our normal life soon afterwards. So, we vacillate in and out of faith until we reach the final stage of walking in the perfect character of Christ. When we walk every day by faith and not by sight, in the perfect disposition of the Redemptive Power of the Cross, the glory of God never leaves us. By faith—faith becomes us. Abraham had become faith. He knew that in life or death, in sacrifice of Isaac and in the new land, that the glory of God was his. You are walking by faith as Abraham did when faith has truly become the "substance of things hoped for, and the evidence of things not seen." By faith believe in God.

Week 8 Day 7

IDENTIFYING WITH CHRIST

*"I have been crucified with Christ and I
no longer live, but Christ lives in me."*

—*GALATIANS 2:20*

"The life I live in the body, I live by faith in the Son of God, who loved me and gave himself for me." Take a moment and really think about how much Christ had to love you to die for you—not simply die but die by crucifixion. For Christ to live in you, you must identify with His love and His crucifixion. Paul said, "I have been crucified with Christ." Paul gave up his right to himself and lost himself in the life of Christ. The thing that we must do is give up our right to ourselves and live by faith in the Savior, Jesus Christ, the Son of God. When you can say that you no longer live, but Christ lives in you, then you have reconciled to sin and sin no longer has any power over you. You are freed from the captivity of sin by the Redemption of the Cross of Christ, and you identify with Christ in His Death.

We can be easily attracted to the celebratory Life and Resurrection of Christ and bask in the glory of the miracles He performed. There was nothing celebratory or glorious about His brutal and traumatic death on the cross, a death resulting in the bones of His pierced body being broken to create blood clots. Christ suffered unfathomable pain under the weight of His own body pressing down against the many blood clots, until He suffocated from the lack of blood carrying oxygen to His brain. We must identify with, not be attracted by the Death of Christ. Identification goes well beyond a temporary and fleeting attraction. When you identify with something, that something becomes a part of you; it lives in you. The Death of Christ must become a part of you; Christ must live in you, through you identifying with His Death. When you come to such a mental and moral decision and absorb the blows that must come to batter you into the shape of the vision, you then no longer live. The instant you give up your right to yourself, you allow the Holy Ghost to have His way in your life and impart to you the perfect character of Christ.

When Christ lives in you, you remain the same natural person you always were, but spiritually you are a new creature.

Your mentality and moral compass are significantly reshaped into God's vision for your life. Supernaturally, you are transfigured in your identification with the Death of Christ. You deny your personal interests and take up your cross and follow Jesus. You exist in the same flesh, but your old way of chasing after worldly things is completely eliminated. When Christ lives in you, you live by faith in the Savior, Jesus Christ, the Son of God. The faith you live by is the faith that Christ imparts to you when He lives in you, through identifying with His Death. Have you been crucified with Christ? Have you given up your right to yourself and you no longer live? Does Christ Jesus live in you? Do you identify with Christ?

THE KNOWLEDGE OF GOOD AND EVIL

"You are free to eat from any tree in the garden; but you must not eat from the tree of the knowledge of good and evil, for when you eat from it you will surely die."

—*GENESIS 2:16-17*

*You will surely die...*With the first act of disobedience to the command of God, Adam and Eve brought death upon all of mankind. Because of their sin, all of mankind is born into sin, and because we are born into sin, we must die to overcome sin. With one act of disobedience, the entire human race fell out of God's good grace and was put out of the Garden of Eden; a place where death did not exist, nor hunger, worry, pain or heartbreak. "The wages of sin is death." Death is what results from a life of sin. Death is what all mankind inherited from the first man and first woman. In spiritual death we suffer tremendously. We hate our neighbors, we anger at family, we do evil and vileness, we molest children, and we murder our bother—Cain killed Abel. Adam and Eve had life in the garden until they brought death upon themselves through blatant disregard for the words God had spoken—"You must not."

You must not...We die a thousand deaths because we ignore the "You must not" of God. Every time we sin, we surely die. Every time we disobey the commands of God, we experience death. The "You must not" of God comes with severe consequences. Women are cursed with the pain of childbirth; men are cursed with hard labor just to eat; and the serpent is cast down on his belly to crawl, all are the severe consequences of Adam and Eve ignoring the "You must not" of God. When we blatantly ignore a command of God, we cause ourselves to suffer death, and the only way to get back to God is through the spiritual rebirth made possible through the death of Christ. Death is the only way back from ignoring the "You must not." Christ had to die, and we must die in Christ, to overcome sin and get back to the full grace of God, which is in the glory of the Kingdom of Christ.

The Knowledge of Good and Evil...So what did Adam and Eve really do that got them placed out of the Garden of

Eden, resulting in an Angel and flaming sword blocking the entrance back in? Adam and Eve, by ignoring the "You must not" of God discovered carnal knowledge. Carnal knowledge is the knowledge of the flesh and sexual desires. They knew they were naked because they had discovered carnal knowledge. The forbidden fruit from the tree of the Knowledge of Good and Evil is a metaphor. The metaphor is Adam and Eve discovered sin through discovering the carnal knowledge of themselves. Carnal knowledge is the Knowledge of Good and Evil. Everything that brings us joy also brings us pain. Sex brings us joy, and it brings us pain. From sex we have children that bring us joy, but children also bring us pain. We experience joy from getting a new job, but because work is a curse, work also brings us pain in the workplace. God made man and woman, which was a good thing. But look at how much pain we have created for God with our disobedience. Imagine the pain God felt when the first two humans He created in His Own image disregarded His "You must not" at the coercing of the Devil through the serpent. The Knowledge of Good and Evil is the fact that God and Satan are battling for our souls. God created us in His image and wants us to do good, righteous, and holy deeds and to follow His commands. Satan wants us to do bad, evil, sinful things and ignore God's commands to make us His followers.

THE JOY THAT COMES IN THE MORNING

*"Weeping may endure for a night,
but joy cometh in the morning."*

—*Psalm 30:5 KJV*

The Knowledge of Good and Evil unveils the hardness and the joys of life. Because of good and evil, we live an existence of duality. God and Satan are battling for our souls. God, Who created us, is trying to save our souls from damnation; and Satan, whom God casted out of heaven, is trying to destroy our souls so we never see the Kingdom of God. In this battle between God and Satan, there is great pain and suffering that we must endure. There is no getting around the throes of life; we must go through sorrow and heartbreak. We must go through trials and tribulations to get to the rejoicing and the glory of the Lord. We must go through weeping for a night to get to the joy that comes in the morning. Our dual existence is experienced in two realms. This cycle of night that turns into morning represents the two realms. Adam and Eve lived in one realm, the Heavenly Realm of God's goodness, until the Serpent introduced them to the Satanic realm of the "kingdom of the air." (*see* Ephesians 2:2) Yes, both good and evil existed in the Garden of Eden. The battle between God and Satan had been going on well before God made Adam and Eve, but with a defiant act of disobedience and their inability to exercise self-denial, Adam and Eve were cast out of God's Heavenly Realm into the Satanic realm of sinfulness. Adam and Eve caused their own sufferings. I cause my own sufferings. You cause your own sufferings. We suffer heartache, pain and sorrow because our blatant disobedience and lack of self-denial angers God, but we are still loved by God because His anger is only temporary. *"For his anger lasts only a moment, but his favor lasts a lifetime."* (Psalm 30:5).

How do we gain favor in the Lord? We gain God's favor through believing in Jesus Christ. *"Whoever believes in the Son has eternal life, but whoever rejects the Son will not see life, for God's wrath remains on him."* (John 3:36). God punishes us with His anger toward us. He loves us so much that He gave His only begotten Son, and to gain the joy that comes in the morning we must believe in Christ, the Lord. We engage in our sinful nature and disobey God, causing ourselves to suffer for a while. This is the weeping we must endure for a night. A night represents the time it takes for us to repent of our sins. Once we repent and call on the name of Jesus, God shows us His love and favor by giving us joy and moments of rejoicing. This represents the morning in the cycle of our dual existence.

Christ Jesus is the Joy that comes in the morning. All throughout the Old Testament there were counts of wretched suffering due to mankind's disobedience and inability to deny oneself of earthly pleasures. There was pleasure in the fruit that Adam and Eve ate. That is precisely the reason the Serpent was able to coerce Eve into tasting the forbidden fruit. The promise of pleasure is why we find it so difficult to deny ourselves. Being addicted to pleasure creates periods of darkness in our lives. But God sent His Son into the world to die for our sins. When Jesus was born, this was mankind's morning of rejoicing, as Christ brought us joy through salvation and sanctification through the Redemptive Power of His death. No matter what we suffer through during the night; heartbreak, divorce, addiction, destitution or sorrow, the morning is always brighter and more joyful because we have the glory and eternal life through Jesus Christ, our Lord and Savior, Who brings us through the night and into the morning.

KEEP YOUR SIGHT SET ON JESUS

*"Then their eyes were opened
and they recognized him, and he
disappeared from their sight."*

—*LUKE 24:31*

We need to learn the secret to keeping our sight set on Jesus. We walk with Christ and talk with Him on our travels and through the throes, but it takes a while before we mature enough in the word of God for our eyes to open up to Who Christ really is. Then suddenly, we recognize Jesus. "Now, I see Him!" This is precisely what happened to

Cleopas and his travel companion on the road to Emmaus. In their dismay and troubled hearts, they walked and talked with Jesus, not knowing that it was Jesus. They were not yet believers; for they still thought of Christ as a Prophet. How many of us walk with Jesus and talk with Jesus, not knowing and believing He is the Son of God? You have heard about Jesus and the great things He has done for others, but He has never revealed Himself to you. But like Cleopas and his companion, you invite Christ into your heart one day, and instantly, over dinner, in the midst of a blessing, or as a witness to His power, you recognize Him as the Son of the Living God. Then, as quickly as He appears to you, Christ disappears from your sight. The sight of Christ brings about an undescriptive and exhilarating joy; it brightens the heart of the believer with burning desire. *"Were not our hearts burning within us?"* (Verse 32). We must learn the secret to keeping Jesus in our sight; for it is the sight of Jesus in our lives, in the midst of our storms, walking on the water, that causes our heart to burn. The heart does not burn when we hear about Jesus. Hearing may get us a little excited; it may even make us shout, but it is seeing Him move in a mighty way, with our own eyes, that causes our heart to burn within us.

Much of our dismay as saints comes with not knowing the secret to keeping Jesus in our sight. Sin is not our issue; Jesus freed us from sin. Our issue is that we allow Jesus to disappear. The reason Jesus disappears is because we do not have the ability to understand the result of our actions until it is too late. If we understood that around every corner, in any given circumstance, at any given moment, all Hell can break loose in our lives, we would never lose sight of Jesus. But because we don't understand the natural laws of antagonism and we naturally believe life is meant to be grand all the time, we never see ourselves as perpetrators of deeds that God condemns.

We must learn to praise God in the morning, in the evening, and in the midnight hour. We are quick to call on Jesus when our hearts are broken, but we are slow to reach out to Him when things are going good in our lives. We act as if the good times will last forever. This is why Jesus disappears. This is why the secret is to learn how to keep your sight on Jesus at all times—in times of both joy and pain. Jesus must be kept in our hearts at all times. If I have a desire for my heart to burn within me with the joy of Jesus Christ, I must learn to abide in Christ and keep Christ abiding in me; otherwise, I will lose sight of Him, and the flame of fire Jesus uses to set my soul on fire will go out. If the Holy Ghost has set your soul on fire, throw all condemnations into the flame, accept all circumstances God has engineered on your behalf. We cannot remain on the mountaintop; we must descend into the valley and make use of the fire God has placed in us. When God opens your eyes, recognize Christ as His Son, and travel the remainder of your days with your spiritual sight set on Jesus, and never turn your eyes away.

THE GREATEST COMMANDMENT

*"Love the Lord your God with all your
heart and with all your soul and with all
your strength and with all your mind."*

—Luke 10:27

Your love is what God wants over anything else you could possibly offer Him. God is not after your simple affection, your acts of good deeds, your kind words or even your obedience. God wants you to love Him with your entire being, with your complete essence, with all your heart, soul, strength and mind. The key here is the word "all." Beware of offering God just a portion of your heart, just a portion of your soul, just a portion of your strength and just a portion of your mind. God is a jealous God. He has absolutely no interest in your half-givens. God wants all of your love.

All your heart... God judges the heart of man, not the deeds. *"Man looks at the outward appearance, but the LORD looks at the heart."* (1 Samuel 16:7). You cannot get into heaven because you look like or act like you are a Christian. You may be able to fool other souls with your outward appearance, but God judges the heart. There are no secret hiding places in the heart. Purity of heart is not about the innocence of man, but rather to whom and what you treasure. It is with the heart you select whom and to what you will serve. God judges the heart in search of; 1 Corinthians 13:4-7. *"Love is patient, love is kind. It does not envy, it does not boast, it is not proud. It is not rude, it is not self-seeking, it is not easily angered, it keeps no record of wrongs. Love does not delight in evil but rejoices with the truth. It always protects, always trusts, always hopes, always perseveres."* If you truly love the Lord with all your heart, this is the love your heart will produce.

All of your soul... With the heart you love the Lord, but it is with the soul that you praise the Holy name of the Lord. *"Praise the Lord, my soul; all my inmost being, praise his holy name."* (Psalm 103:1). You are to praise God and be thankful always, in all circumstances with all your soul. You are mind, body and soul; and God wants you to give all of yourself to Him in praise and worship; for He is worthy to be praised. He gave His only begotten Son so that you could be saved by the Redemption of the Cross of Christ. Palm 59:16 says, *"But I will sing of your strength, in the morning I will sing of your love; for you are my fortress, my refuge in times of trouble."* God wants you to praise Him with all your mind, body and soul in the morning and in the evening, because you know He loves you and protects you.

*All of your strength…*Ecclesiastes 9:10 says; "Whatever your hand finds to do, do it with all your might." When your hand finds the work the Lord has purposed you for, God wants you to do it with all of your strength. You are to use every ounce of talent, intellect, and human endowment the Lord has bestowed upon you in carrying out the work of the Lord. Your work is evidence of your love for God.

*All of your mind…*In loving Him, God wants all of your mind focused on the things of Ecclesiastes 9:10; *"Finally, brothers, whatever is true, whatever is noble, whatever is right, whatever is pure, whatever is lovely, whatever is admirable—if anything is excellent or praiseworthy—think about such things."*

THE MOST INTRICATE RELATIONSHIP IN THE UNIVERSE

*"The friend who attends the bridegroom
waits and listens for him, and is full of joy
when he hears the bridegroom's voice."*

—*JOHN 3:29*

The manners, kindness and generosity of the friends of the bride and groom should never take attention away from the bride and groom on their wedding day; after all, it is the bride and groom's wedding day, and all attention should be focused on them. At a wedding, no one should seek to deprive the bride and groom of their glory. Everyone at the wedding must decrease, so the bride and groom may increase. Righteousness and holiness in the name of the Lord, likewise, should never attract attention away from the Bridegroom—Jesus Christ. John the Baptist fully understood just how intricate the relationship was between him and Christ. It is a very complicated and delicate line to walk when you are the friend of the bridegroom. You must go before the Bridegroom, but you must also never attract any attention away from the Bridegroom. Paul says it this way in 2 Corinthians 2:18: *"For it is not the one who commends himself who is approved, but the one whom the Lord commends."* The friend of Christ should never commend himself or herself. If my righteousness and holiness is not bringing others to Christ, it is not righteousness and holiness in God's order, but an apparatus that will lead souls away from Christ. The saint must be careful to present Christ, and to boast only in the Lord. "Let him who boasts, boast only in the Lord." If you boast about yourself and all the things God has done for you, and never boast about Christ, you will cause others to exalt you and minimize Christ. If you are increasing and receiving all of the accolades, you are not being a true friend to the Bridegroom.

In order to properly maintain respect and loyalty within the most intricate relationship in the entire universe, Christians have to be keenly aware of moral character and natural disposition in our relationship with Christ. Putting the intricacies of our relationship with Christ in proper order is the most important act of Christianity. It is more important than our obedience to Christ. Yes, denying ourselves pleasures, attention and accolades is more important than obedience to God's commands. We must acknowledge, pay homage to, and protect the integrity of the order of our relationship with Christ. "He must become greater; I must become less." It is a very intricate and delicate relationship to have the responsibility to go out and excite the crowd for the coming of someone who is greater than you. Even in our own household and personal relationships, Christ must be greater than we are to our spouse, children, family and friends. There is very seldom a time in which we must obey a command from God. Obedience is not a daily proposition, but the relationship with Christ is an everyday, all day, proposition. We must fight to keep all things away that have the possibility of coming between us and our intricate relationship with Jesus Christ. Christ is our way, our truth, and our life. We can only get to the Father through Him. We can only get to the Father of the Bridegroom if we have been a proper friend to the Bridegroom. The life of a Christian is more about the upkeep of the most intricate relationship with Christ, than it is about the mental and moral concentration of our emotions toward obedience to Christ. Let nothing invade your life in Christ, and Christ in you. Be a friend to the Bridegroom.

Week 9 Day 6

LORD, YOU ARE GREATER

"He must become greater; I must become less."

—JOHN 3:30

"*The one who comes from above is above all.*" (Verse 31). The Authority of God, the Father, is Supreme; He is above all, and His purpose must rule supreme in our lives. That was the message John the Baptist conveyed to his disciples. John stated that we are from the earth and can only do and speak earthly things. John the Baptist preached that there was One Who was coming that is greater than he was, because He is sent from above—from God. As great a servant of the Lord as John was, baptizing all nations in the name of the Father, the Son, and the Holy Ghost, John also recognized that Christ Jesus was far greater than he was. "The thongs of whose sandals I am not worthy to untie." Behind every word we speak; after every thought we project; in front of every action we take; and beside every place we go, Christ Jesus must become greater, and we must become less. If you project yourself as someone that another person cannot live without, you are pretending to be greater than God, and you are out of order with God's purpose. As servants to the Most High, we have a responsibility to serve Christ just as "the friend who attends to the bridegroom." When you operate in proper order with the purpose of God, every relationship you have with other souls is an evangelism. When you see other souls being brought to Christ in your evangelism, you then know Christ is becoming greater, and you are becoming less.

In a marriage, souls should be brought to Christ. Neither the husband, nor the wife, should ever project himself or herself as being more important than Christ. Christ must rule Supreme in marriages, as in all relationships. Otherwise, God will not be able to work out His purpose. In a parent-child relationship, parents should bring their children to Christ, not projecting themselves as the highest authority. God's purpose for our children should reign supreme over our personal interests and desires concerning our children. Instead of projecting parental privilege over our children, spousal rights over our wives and husbands, or false supremacy in our friendships and love affairs, we should insure we are not stumbling blocks that intend to prevent the pain and suffering in life; but rather pray and ask God to allow His purpose for those we love to grow in the Light of the Glory of the Kingdom until there is no power or force on earth or in heaven that can separate those we love from the Love of Christ Jesus, our Lord. Our love and affection for other souls should never be so great that it causes others to fall or even stumble in their relationship with the Lord. "Your Purpose, Lord. Not mine."

Instead of being the friend to the Bridegroom, we have a way of putting our wants and desires before the will and purpose of God. We sympathize and empathize, and we beg and plead; we lean on the heart strings of others until we get our way. We prevent others from getting to Christ because we make ourselves essential and necessary. Being essential and necessary is not evangelism; it creates counter narratives to the greater purpose of God. Beware of coercing other souls to follow the wrong path; but be quick to celebrate the throes of the right path. John the Baptist was rejoicing when he said: "That joy is mine, and it is now complete. He must become greater; and I must become less." John was extremely joyful to hear the voice of Jesus baptizing and preaching on the other side of the Jordan. Likewise, we must rejoice when we hear the voice of Christ saving souls in our homes, communities and friendships. The greatest joy of a servant of Christ is when you are no longer relevant. Christ has become greater.

TIME AND SEASON

*"There is a time for everything, and a
season for every activity under heaven."*

—ECCLESIASTES 3:1

God has ordered the heavens and the earth, and time refers to the fact that everything God has planned will come to be. God is in complete control of time, His time and ours. Season refers to the limited time God has allotted to us for completing the activities He has purposed our lives for. Because our activities have a purpose, they also have a season within which they must be done. When God calls us into season, we must complete our task on His time. Many of us are not instinctively in sync seasonally with God's spiritual timing. In this sense, season is not a condition of time, it is a condition of our awareness and readiness. When God says it is time, we must be aware and ready to instantly do the work of the Lord. God's timing is always perfect; but the issue comes down to our willingness to act in the immediacy—Right now! We must be ready and willing to act with all our might, whether we feel up to it or not. The work is never for our benefit. Our season is for the benefit of others. How we perform in our season determines if our name will be written in the Book of Life. We spend our lives engaged in meaningless activities, hindering the maturing of our fruit for our season. If we engage only in what we feel up to, many of us would never mature into fruit that would be of use to God. Some have fruit that has become rotten because it was not picked and put to use when God called you to be in season. Your spirit is dilapidated and feeble. This happens when saints refuse to act in commonplaces in common ways, waiting to be called to do something grand and fantastic. Our fruit is of daily benefit to others. It is in the valley that God squeezes the nectar out of us so others can taste the sweetness of the juice our mature fruit produces. Are you willing to allow God to make you the perfect fruit with the sweetest nectar for others to drink? The proof that we are rightly related to God is our willingness to be pressed-down and squeezed for the benefit of others whenever and wherever God calls us into season.

If we fall into this notion of waiting for a rare and grandiose moment to allow God to squeeze out our nectar, then we run the risk of our fruit becoming rotten and decrepit, of no use to God. All fruit has a season. The time in which we can put forth a peak performance has a season. The greatest athletes have only a short season in which they can perform at a world-class level. The same is the with the Christian saint. When the Spirit of the Lord brings you to the starting-block and fires the gun, this is the very moment in which the Spirit of God is pouring into you His spiritual insight. This is the very season in which God is inspiring you to run your best race. The race is a gift from the Lord Himself. You cannot choose the race you have to run or the time your race is set to start. God is the organizer, the timekeeper and the official over the season we are called to perform in. You can't wait for the inspiration that comes from the rare opportunities in the big season, you must remain inspired by your relationship with Christ Jesus, your Redeemer, in the small season. Beware of praising the big season of your best moments, and remember, the race does not always go to the swift. Your season is not about winning, but rather about bringing souls to Christ. It is not whether you win or lose, but how you compete that spreads the gospel of Christ.

Week 10 Day 1

EVERYTHING IS MEANINGLESS!

"Meaningless! Meaningless! Utterly meaningless! Everything is meaningless."

—*ECCLESIASTES 1:2*

What are we doing here on earth? Everything we put our minds to and anything our hands touch is meaningless. The only thing we can do that has any chance of possessing an iota of value and meaning is to chase after God's Heart. If you are not focused on pleasing God with your every thought and with every act, then whatever else you are engaged in is absolutely meaningless to God! Your education is meaningless!

The wise will die just as the unwise. Being a nice person has no value in life. The sun rises and falls for the just and the unjust. Your earthly accomplishments are worthless! Everything you do will be forgotten shortly after you die. The only ones who will remember you will be your family and closest friends, and even they will remember you only for a little while. Therefore, your efforts to build things on earth are of no use to God. Your relationship with other human souls, your spouse and family, will not save your soul or be of any benefit to your campaign to get into heaven. Only Jesus is the Way, the Truth, and the Life. No one gets to the Father, except through Christ. So, what are we doing here on earth? Everything is meaningless! It doesn't matter if you are the President of the United States or the President or CEO of a fortune 500 corporation or any other major organization. Your station in life cannot save your soul, therefore it is meaningless! It doesn't matter if the whole world knows your name or what your celebrity status is to others. Your popularity is meaningless! God doesn't care if you were born in a big house or an outhouse. God doesn't care what your zip code is or the size of your bank account. The only thing of value to you or God is your relationship with the Redeemer. Are you rightly related to Christ Jesus? No other question on earth has any worth, because your salvation is the only thing you can gain on this earth that has any meaning whatsoever. Everything else, everything else, everything else is meaningless! Meaningless! Meaningless! Meaningless!

The two thieves who were crucified, one on each side of Christ, had accomplished nothing meaningful in their lives, when compared to basic human standards. By all standards, they had lived lives of crime and sin. I imagine they were unlearned, unwise, weak, slow and unbrilliant. None of that mattered. If they were all together something else, clergymen or popular singers, perhaps that would not have added any value to their souls. All that would have mattered was the relationship they established with the Lord Jesus before they died. The thieves had not performed a lifetime of services unto the Lord; they had traveled the world saving souls. Yet, their names are written in the Book in the Kingdom of God. That is all that matters for us all. Is your name written in the Book of Life? If your name is not written in heaven, then you have wasted your entire time on earth attempting to have a meaningful life. But, if given the opportunity to choose Christ, even if it is the last thing you do before taking your last breath, choose Him with all your heart and mind, and your time on earth will have great meaning.

"What does man gain from all his labor at which he toils under the sun?" (Verse 3). There is nothing meaningful under the sun. The only thing that matters about this life is gaining salvation, making it into the procession of saints, marching into the Kingdom of God, and sitting with Christ at the right hand of His Throne. That is the only thing that has meaning, the only thing!

GOD FAVORS YOU

*"Look at the birds of the air; they do not
sow or reap or store away in barns, and
yet your heavenly Father feeds them. Are
you not much more valuable than they?"*

—*Matthew 6:26*

The natural life of man is very interesting when you consider the things we have the propensity to worry about and stress over. We seldom stop to consider just how much God favors us. A simple glance at nature around us signals that God is prepared to take care us, because He values us much more than He does the things in nature. *"So do not worry saying, 'What shall we eat?' or 'What shall we drink?' or*

'What shall we wear?'" (Matthew 6:31). If He feeds the birds, He will feed you. If He clothes the lilies of the field, He will clothe you as well. We get too caught up in what others have. Instead of recognizing God's favor on us, we compare our small house to someone else's larger house. As children of the Most-High, sin really isn't our issue. Our issue is uncontrollable want. When God blesses us with a house, we want a bigger house. When God blesses us with a spiritual blessing, we want bigger spiritual blessings. This incessant wanting of more has the ability to negate the blessings that we do have. If you missed the message in the miracle of the feeding of the multitude, or the message in the miracle of turning water into wine, then you probably are not aware of just how much God favors you. The miracle in feeding the multitude with a few fish and a few pieces of bread was not about multiplying the quantity of fish and bread available, but rather about everyone spiritually adjusting their ability to be satisfied with what is available. There is always an abundance when you are able to be satisfied with a little. Jesus did not ask the wedding attendees what type of wine they wanted; He simply made wine and said, "If you are drinking, you best drink up." God's favor is not found in the brand name of the clothing, the size of the house, or in the quality of the wine. His favor is in the fact that you do not have to worry about having clothing, a home, or wine. Irrespective of brand name, size or quantity, God's provisions are enough.

God's grace upon you is His favor manifested in you. If through grace, God appoints you over His flock, don't count

194

the flock for the purpose of comparing how many you have-more or less than another shepherd. Simply recognize that through God's grace you are the shepherd and not the sheep. Recognize the favor manifested in your small house and in being in your right mind, because through grace God could have made you homeless and out of your mind. You have to recognize the favor of God in the small things before you can fully appreciate the rare occasions when the big things come your way. If you woke up this morning, you have God's favor. If your children are healthy, you have God's favor. If you are a living dog and not a dead lion, you have God's favor. You may have a chronic illness, a broken heart, or a soul filled with sorrow; but recognize that God still favors you.

Don't allow the Devil to hinder your relationship with God because you may not have what others have. Adjust the threshold of your ability to be satisfied to align with the provisions of God's blessings. Just a few fish and a few pieces of bread really are enough. Whatever the wine is that God is serving, let it satisfy your needs. Irrespective of the description of your circumstances or the quantity in the talents you have been given, know that God favors you. Make His Way your way, keep to His teachings, and His grace will always be upon you in a favorable manner. If you find yourself being dissatisfied in life, revisit the miracle of the feeding of the multitude and consider the lilies of the field and the birds in the air. God favors you!

SUPREME DEVOTION

"Take your son, your only son, Isaac, whom
you love, and go to the region of Moriah.
Sacrifice him there as a burnt offering on
one of the mountains I will tell you about."

—*GENESIS 22:2*

Being wholly devoted to God does not and should not mean that you will do anything. God does not ask us to do just anything. He expects us to obey His commands. There is a big difference. Being willing to do anything makes you a fanatic, not a saint. God wants you to be true to Him and have faith in Him in all circumstances, including being willing to sacrifice the people and the things that you cherish the most. Staying true and being faithful to God in all circumstances is not being fanatical, it's being supremely devoted to the nature and interests of God. Supreme devotion is asking God what His interests are in every situation He places you in and acting without doubt on what you believe God's interests are. When you love your children, as Abraham loved Isaac, you must allow God's interests to have a superior position to your interests. We cannot love our children so much that God's interests run inferior to ours. When God brings us to the precipice of trust and faith in Him, it is not a test, even though the Devil convinces us that it is, it is God's process of bringing us into a better relationship with Him. In a better relationship, we gain better knowledge, greater faith, and deeper trust in God through Jesus Christ. We gain a better relationship with God only through ordeals that require us to demonstrate a supreme devotion to His Supreme Authority. You have heard the familiar refrain: "No pain, not gain." Supreme devotion often is accompanied by great suffering and extreme sacrifice; otherwise, there would be very little to gain. Those who have demonstrated the greatest devotion to the truths about God tend to be the ones who have the greatest knowledge of God.

We all have developed our own beliefs about the true nature of God. Many of these beliefs are untested because they have yet to be taken through an ordeal that requires you to leave the city of your comfort and go into the wilderness of uncertainty. It is in the wilderness of our uncertainty where God directs us to make the great climb up to Him, and then He places us in an extreme circumstance. In the throes of spiritual extremity is precisely when God brings us to the threshold of gaining a better relationship with Him. We must decide if we will step through God's threshold of knowledge demonstrating faith and trust in Him, or if we will not. God is not seeking fanatics; He is seeking saints who are seeking a greater knowledge of His kingdom, saints who are painstakingly chasing with a supremely devoted spirit after His heart. "No pain, no gain."

God does not remove people from our lives, especially our own children, because we love them too much. That is not the nature of God. Now, God will use your love for another person to bring you into a better relationship with Him or remove people who are a hinderance to you. (*see* Psalm 37 and Deuteronomy 28). Killing your own child in a burnt offering will not bring you into a better relationship with God. It will only make you a fanatic. The great attribute of being supremely devoted, as Abraham was, is you are prepared to obey God in all circumstances, even if your obedience causes you to go against something you previously believed. God wants us to have a great knowledge of Him. Ultimately, He is trying to get us to a place of supreme devotion to Him.

Week 10 Day 4

IN THE
CHARACTER OF
GOD

"To the faithful, you show yourself faithful,
to the blameless, you show yourself blameless,
to the pure you show yourself pure, but to
the crooked you show yourself shrewd."

—PSALM 18:25-26

Insight into God's will and purpose is determined by the character of the saint. If you take on the perfect character of Jesus Christ, you will see the perfect character of Christ in God's will and purpose. If you take on a character that is contrary to the character of Christ, God will present Himself to you as hard and shrewd. We often misinterpret God's command because we are not in the character of God. God can break us from our common mistakes concerning His will, only by taking us through an ordeal that alters our innate character, thus aligning our purpose with His purpose. God did not intend for Abraham to kill Isaac in a burnt offering, but God had to take Abraham through a character changing ordeal to break Abraham from a traditional way in which he saw God. God had to bring Abraham to a higher level of faith and to a higher level of understanding, so that God could show Himself to Abraham in a higher level of faith and understanding. God takes us through spiritual auspices to reshape us into the proper aspect of being blameless, so He can show Himself to us as being blameless. God has to transform our character into His character before He can reveal His true nature to us. If we are not in the faithful, blameless, and pure character of God, God cannot reveal Himself to us as faithful, blameless, and pure.

We can only understand character from the perspective of the character we have also developed into. If I have a sinful nature and a corrupt heart, I cannot receive God as blameless and pure. I can only perceive His shrewd and condemning nature. To get to God's goodness and mercy, I must go through a transforming of my character. I must be given a clean spirit, which is a gift from the Holy Ghost. I cannot pray for a character transformation; the Holy Ghost must ask God on my behalf through intercessory prayer. Abraham did not pray to God to send him the vision to take his son to a mountain to kill him. The Holy Spirit intervened on behalf of Abraham, and through the ordeal of a spiritual crisis, Abraham's character was transformed. Abraham gained a greater knowledge of the nature of God. This is why we must be born again. A sinner has no comprehension of the knowledge of the nature of God. It is not until we turn our lives over to Christ and connect with the perfect character of Christ that can God show us His Godly nature. Faithfulness, blamelessness, and purity means absolutely nothing to a sinner.

If you remain true to the nature of God, God will transform your character, cleanse your spirit, and pull you up into a greater knowledge of Himself. The pulling up of God into a higher spiritual character always involves leaving bad habits, misinterpretations, and old traditions behind. The character that God is trying to connect you to is already inside you. He is not putting anything inside you; in transformation of character, the Holy Spirit is already in you; God is simply taking something out so you can get to what is already there. God takes the sin out, so you can get to the righteousness that is already in you. God removes the corruption from your heart, so all that is left is the purity that was always there. God rips out all the doubt and second guessing, so you see the blamelessness that was put in before you were born again. God gets rid of all the tradition, so you have only faithfulness left. God brings out His character.

IN COMPLETE UNITY

"I in them and you in me. May they be brought to complete unity to let the world know that you sent me and have loved them even as you have loved me."

—*John 17:23*

Christianity is the spiritual atonement in which we become one with Christ, as Christ is one with His Father. If Christ is in you and He is in God, then you are in complete unity—You, the Son, and the Father are One. You cannot be in complete unity with Christ and God if you are only seeking great things for yourself. Christianity is not a blessings exposition; it is coming into greater knowledge of God and the glory of His kingdom. God is not interested in our constant requests for yet another blessing. God wants us to desire to know Him through a complete unity with Christ, not simply chasing after His many gifts. His blessings come and go with the wind, but being rightly related to God lasts forever. If you ever get a great gift, it is a very rare thing; but a rightly related relationship with Christ can be a commonplace thing. We simply need to seek the kingdom of God, and not the gifts of God. Complete unity with God has to be the goal, not simply attaining earthly blessings.

Yes, God does allow us to come to Him and ask for whatever we want, but the mistake is in thinking you can ask for things that do not align with God's will. You cannot. We must ask for things that align with God's interest and purpose. How we learn what God's interest and purpose are, is by getting into complete unity with Him. When we are one with Christ, we know the right things are to ask for. If you have only come to the point of asking God for great gifts, you have never gotten to the point of coming into alignment with Christ. Alignment with Christ begins with abandoning oneself to Christ. Until you abandon yourself, you cannot align with Christ. Until you align with Christ, you cannot unite with Christ. You must seek the Lord with all your heart and soul. God already knows what you want, so do not bother asking for it. Seek His kingdom first, then all things will be given unto you. When you become aligned with the Atonement of Jesus Christ through the Power of the Redemption, you will stop praying selfishly for yourself. You will start praying for the transformation into the perfect character of Christ. That is when you know that your prayers are along the proper line with God.

Are you seeking God's heart, or are you selfishly seeking great things for yourself? Your Father knows your every need and want. What exactly should you be praying for? You should be praying that God shows you His perfect character, His true nature, so you can get to know Him better and better. The knowledge of our Lord God Almighty, our Savior and Redeemer, is precisely what brings you into complete unity with Him. If God does not bring you into complete unity with Him, it is because you have not gotten to the point of completely abandoning yourself to Christ. If that is the matter at hand, you must ask yourself what is holding you back. You must ask God to free you from whatever is keeping you from abandoning yourself to Christ. There is something you are not quite ready to give up in your life. You are not ready to deny yourself to your own self-interests. Until you are ready, God cannot baptize you with the Holy Spirit, and it is the Holy Spirit that brings you into complete unity with the Father, through your relationship with the Son. God is not focused on your happiness; He is focused on making you one with Him and Christ. Then your happiness becomes His priority.

Week 10 Day 6

YOUR COMPLETE
LIFE

*"Should you then seek great things for
yourself? Seek them not. For I will bring
disaster on all people...but wherever you
go I will let you escape with your life."*

—*JEREMIAH 45:5*

You will live a complete life. This is the undeniable truth
to those who live in complete unity with the Lord and
trust Him with all your heart and soul—"I will let you escape
with your life." This is not a secret. This is knowledge gained
by being one with the Savior. There is nothing more to want

than life itself. God says, "I will bring disaster," but your life will always be intact. As a sinner or a saint, you will escape the disasters of life . To all who have life, God gives you complete life. No one lives a partial life. Even if your life is not everything you hoped it would be, or your life ends suddenly in despair, your life will be complete. There is no benefit to spending your life asking God for great things. God says, "Seek them not." This means He is going to bring disaster and destroy everything on earth, the great things and the not-so-great things. Many of us are emphatically wanting the greater things in life. Why? These temporary things will come to pass, but your life is permanent. Everyone will have an afterlife. Where you spend eternity depends on the relationship you build with God in this life. If you spend this life chasing after the wind, hoping it will blow great blessings from God in your direction, all you will do is collect things that the next great wind will blow away and destroy. We cannot take anything from this life with us into the next life. Therefore, let the great chase of this life be the chase after God's heart. There is nothing more grandiose than the life you can have hidden in God with Christ. The oneness with Christ in God is the complete life. A life where God will allow you to escape all disasters intact.

Are you ready to completely abandon yourself to Christ and become one with the Lord in God? If so, then give no further consideration to chasing after the great things that God is going to destroy. Instead, focus on the quality of your relationship with Christ and the aligning of your character with the perfect character of the Almighty. The test of whether you are ready for a life of oneness with the Lord is in what you are actually asking God for. Abandonment to Christ means you have trust and faith in God. You trust that all your needs and wants will be satisfied without having to ask. When you trust and have faith in God, you will stop asking God for personal blessings. Instead, you will ask God to give you a better knowledge of God Himself. The very instant you abandon yourself to Christ, you will give no further consideration to earthly things, and immediately your life is complete with Christ in God. As a child of God, we have the privilege of asking God for anything. But there is a far greater privilege in having a life with Christ that is so exquisite, that you never have to ask Him for a thing. In such a righteous union with the Lord, all your needs and wants are satisfied.

You must get to a state in this life where you know and trust that God has you covered in every situation. You must have faith that you will escape every disaster with your life intact. This is the simplicity of God in obedience to abandonment. Keep things simple with the Lord and live a complete life.

Week 10 Day 7

THE LOVE OF GOD IS FOR CERTAIN

"How great is the love the Father has lavished on us, that we should be called children of God! And that is what we are!"

—1 JOHN 3:1

It is human nature to doubt things about ourselves and about life itself. How we exist in the natural universe and our actual supernatural connection to the Lord, God Almighty is uncertain at times. But this form of uncertainty drives us to get answers that are critical to who we are; therefore, uncertainty and a certain level of doubt can be positive.

As humans we tend to approach life as if there is some particular destination we should be striving for. We chase success, goals, and arbitrary ends, but there are no spiritual ends that God has given us to reach for. Such endeavors are strictly human endeavors. God does not care about our goals or our will to succeed in life. All He cares about is whether or not we are certain about the love He has lavished upon us. In fact, the only certainty of a spiritual life is the fact that God loves us. Chasing some arbitrary, meaningless goal or some preconceived, worthless human pursuit is not the nature of a life in Christ. We are children of the Most-High God! The nature of the spiritual life in Christ Jesus is that we are certain who our Father is. We may be uncertain about many things, but we are certain that God loves us. We can question our abilities, and we may have doubt in our interpretations. We may even be uncertain concerning our walk, but if we are not sure concerning whether we are a child of God, that is because we have never known we were a child of God.

By nature, we look for auspice signs that God is real. We even deploy our natural intellect and our various experiments with knowledge to determine what we believe we know. The natural life cannot provide any credible conclusions concerning the nature of God. In fact, from a natural perspective, it stands to reason that we would doubt God's love. How can God love a race of people who crucified His Son, especially when there is not one amongst us that would do as Christ did for the entire human race. *"Greater love has no one than this, that he lay down his life for his friends."* (John 15:13). There should be absolutely no doubt that God loves us. He sent His only Son, and Christ died for our sins, knowing no one on earth would have done the same for Him. We can be certain spiritually, while we are uncertain naturally, that we are children of the Living God in Christ Jesus.

Also, be certain that Jesus is going to return. We are uncertain as to how and when He will return, but He is coming back. Until He returns, He abides in us, and we in Him. *"Those who obey his commands live in him, and he in them. And this is how we know that he lives in us. We know it by the spirit he gave us."* (1 John 3:24). This is what gives the saint that great deal of certainty concerning the love and the coming of Christ; Christ gave us His spirit. We may not be able to explain it to others, but we know when Christ has given us His spirit and made in us a new creature. The way others will know is by Christ giving them His spirit. You cannot ask for it; it is a gift from the Holy Ghost. Remain loyal to the love of the Lamb of God, for He is coming back for those He loves and those who love Him back. *"If you obey my commands, you will remain in my love, just as I have obeyed my Father's commands and remain in his love."* (John 15:10). The love of Christ Jesus is the only thing that is certain, and you should be certain that you don't want to live without His love.

Week 11 Day 1

THE NATURE
OF LOVE

*"Now these three remain: faith, hope and
love. But the greatest of these is love."*

—1 CORINTHIANS 13:13

The nature of love: *"Love is patient, love is kind. It does not
envy, it does not boast, it is not proud. It is not rude, it is not
self-seeking, it is not easily angered, it keeps no record of wrongs.
Love does not delight in evil but rejoices with the truth. It always
protects, always trusts, and always hopes, always perseveres. Love
never fails."* (1 Corinthians 13:4-8). Love is the most natural
aspect of our lives. Love is also the greatest human attribute.

It can't be fabricated out of artificial emotions or manufactured in a lab. Real love is 100% natural. Love is the most amazing feeling one can experience or express. The essence of love as Paul describes love cannot be calculated or measured, nor is it certain. Love is not magical; meaning love does not automatically, at the waving of a wand, make envy, hate, evil desires, anger or self-interests disappear. Love does not magically produce trust, hope and perseverance. The perfect standards of the character of Christ Jesus are the bedrock of the nature of love Paul describes. Without the Spirit of the Lord dwelling in you, the true nature of love cannot spontaneously erupt out of your human nature. If love is somehow supernatural, then it is the Spirit of Christ that makes it possible for humans to engage this supernatural element of life. When the supernatural Spirit of Christ is having His way with us, the nature of love will be natural in us, and we will spontaneously, without any sort of premeditation, exude love that is patient, kind, trusting, hopeful and never fails. When the Spirit of God is in you, everything you do will have an element of His love, naturally.

There are various Spirits of love, and they all spring from God Himself. God is the source of the nature of love. Love is not a human creation; it is a divine intervention. *"God has poured out his love into our hearts by the Holy Spirit, whom he has given us."* (Romans 5:5). Love is a gift from the Holy Spirit, and a sign that Jesus Christ is having His way in your life, if you have become the nature of love. Without realizing it, you stop delighting in others' misfortunes. You stop recording wrongs and start forgiving them. Without any consideration for self-interest, you are no longer envious of others, you cease boasting and do away with pride. That's real love. That's the nature of love in Christ.

If we have to try to prove to someone that we love them, then we really don't love them; for love is the most natural of all human emotions. It is either there, or it isn't. Again, love cannot be faked. If you are thinking of love, then you are faking love. We cannot fake our love of Christ. If we believe there is a method for proving to God that we love Him, then our love for God is not real. The demonstration of our love for God and Christ is that there is no premeditated thought that goes into it. Our love for the Almighty bursts out of us in the most phenomenal ways, without us realizing it. It is as natural as breathing. It is as spontaneous as looking up and recognizing the sun, and saying, "Wow! Thank you, Lord for this day!" This is clear evidence that God is manifesting Himself in us for the benefit of others. God is allowing His Light to shine through us in the form of the most amazing love in the universe—Godly Love.

Week 11 Day 2

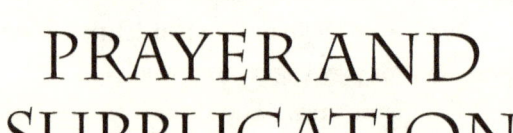

PRAYER AND SUPPLICATION

"Pray in the Spirit on all occasions
will all kinds of prayers and requests.
With this in mind, be alert and always
keep on praying for all the saints."

—*EPHESIANS 6:18*

We should pray always, staying alert for tricks and schemes of the Evil One. Prayer is not simply reaching up to God; prayer and supplication are the means by which we become rightly related to God in the Spirit. God is Spirit, we can only communicate with Him in the Spirit and through the Spirit. God never comes down to us; we must go up to Him. There is no means to physically getting up to God; therefore, the Holy Ghost is the intercessory by which our prayers and requests are taken up to God. As we engage in intercession with the Holy Spirit, we learn that our obedience to God comes at a cost to ourselves and to others. The cost is always more than we anticipate. God is not only a jealous God; He is also a very demanding God. The harm comes in the form of our requests, our supplication, in which we ask God not to make our devotion to Him so costly to those around us. We pray to God in the Spirit for faith, trust and understanding, and then we make a request to remain loyal to our friends; or we at least ask God to be a little lenient when it comes to our family and friends. Our prayers and our requests must be in the Spirit, and they must be in the line of God's interests. Before we engage in prayer and supplication, we must first inquire from God concerning His interests in others and ourselves. Then when we go to God in spiritual prayer and supplication, our prayers and requests are in proper alignment with the will of God. "Your will Lord, not mine."

Intercessory prayer and supplication are not possible if we are not sure of God's interests, His will, and what He has purposed our lives for. God is not going to answer prayers and requests that do not align with His will and purpose for our lives. So, there is really no point in requesting God to show sympathy for yourself or for others. God expects our obedience and our loyalty, and there is absolutely no relief from that line of expectation. Obedience and loyalty to the Most-High establishes a relationship with God that is vital to intercessory prayer and supplication. When we are able to identify with what God has for His children, we become rightly connected to His interests in ourselves and others. Without such vivid identification, prayer and supplication is futile. Such futility is not a conduction of sin, but rather the result of having an empathetic and sympathetic spirit. Your prayers and supplication can only reach God by way of having a godly Spirit. We must remain in sync and rightly related to God at all times, or we risk destroying the critical connection through which God allows us to communicate directly with Him. Otherwise, the Holy Ghost Himself must intervene on our behalf.

Prayer and supplication are not about your selfish interest in great things. Your request along the line of self-pity is not the path to God's heart. We are the same people who crucified Jesus. God has no sympathy for us or our issues. A life of obedience and loyalty to God through Christ is the only way to the Father. Keep your interests identified with God's interests. Keep your interests in others identified with God's interest in them. Do these things and your prayers and requests will always be rightly related to the will of the Lord. "Holy! Holy! Holy! God you are worthy to be praised!"

Week 11 Day 3

IT'S NOT ABOUT YOU

"Now it is God who has made us for this purpose and has given us the Spirit as a deposit, guaranteeing what is to come."

—2 CORINTHIANS 5:5

When you are first called to God's service, you and others around you can see the presence of God upon you. Soon afterwards, God's presence upon you disappears out of plain sight. God leaves you in such a manner that you are left feeling abandoned by Him. You may even start to resent the odd look He leaves on you. Suddenly, you begin to feel sorrow and self-pity; but it's not about you. It never was. God made you for His purpose. Your trials and tribulations are to make you something God can use in the valley, and when you get to the valley, God intends for you to work in obscurity. God does not want you to be seen. God wants others to see only what He has been manifested in you. All glory, honor and praise belong to the Lord. Spiritual obscurity is not a place you go to naturally, for naturally you want to be seen. But it's not about you. It's all about Jesus. You must do the work of a servant of the Lord even when you cannot see God. All that is vital is that the love of God has been manifested in you, and God's love in you is visible to others. Sainthood is not about living a celebrity lifestyle, but rather becoming less so Christ can become greater. If you go about your work in the name of the Lord in an effort to become necessary to others, then God is not big enough in the life of those God has placed in your path. A saint that labors for attention, fortune or fame does not have the true nature of God's love and is of no use to God. You are merely human. While you have been given the gift of the Holy Spirit, you are not transformed into anything that isn't human. The gift of the Holy Spirit is given to you as a deposit so that God can guarantee His work will get done, according to His will and purpose. You are purposed to do the work of God in a world that is hostile and inundated daily with extreme turmoil and destructive behavior. The Spirit of God gives you an infinitely greater power to withstand the onslaughts of evil, but this infinitely greater power is for God's use, not yours.

God sent you from above, reborn in His Spirit, and inspires you with great moments of delight and tantalizing events that create emotional bliss in you. These are God's "WOW" moments while we dwell temporarily on His spiritual mountaintop, but God did not make you for the mountaintop. He made you for the valley. You were made something on the mountain that is of use only in the valley. If you try to return to the mountain and escape the turmoil in the valley, it is a sign that it is not God that you really want. It is a sign that you are out for your own gain. But it's not about you. It's about the work of the Lord. You cannot become addicted to the emotional bliss of rare moments. If you do, you will chase these moments, instead of chasing after God's heart. God may never bring you to the mountaintop ever again. He has already made you everything to satisfy His purpose for your life. Now, God wants you to walk by faith in the valley of the brokenhearted and spiritually diseased. "We live by faith, not by sight." You must walk in the Light of the faith in Christ Jesus, even when you can't see the face of God. Don't live for the rare moments on the mountaintop. Don't pray for signs and blessings for yourself. Love with the nature of God upon you, and let everything you do be about Jesus, not about you.

THE PERSISTENCE OF FAITH

"Yes, Lord, but even the dogs eat the crumbs that fall from their master's table."

—*MATTHEW 15:27*

Faith is indifferent to circumstance; faith has the persistence of an immensely determined woman trying to save her daughter's life. The knowledge of the power, goodness and mercy of God is the source of faith, because it imparts a moral persistence. The Canaanite woman knew of the power of the Almighty. She also knew the food of the Lord was not for her because she was not an Israelite. But her faith was persistent, and she endured. She told the Lord that she was not interested in taking food from His chosen people, but she would prayerfully, thankfully and faithfully accept the crumbs from His table. Her persistence proved to Christ that she had immense faith in the power of His crumbs. *"Woman, you have great faith. Your request is answered."* (Verse 28). The woman's persistence of faith delivered her daughter from her demonic possession. The woman endured through her trials because she had a vision of God in all His glory. A person with a vision of God is devoted to God Himself, not to the particular cause that gave rise to calling on God. You always know when the persistence of faith has brought you to the vision of God because of the inspiration that comes along with it. The Canaanite woman was highly inspired by the vision of God in her neighborhood. When we see the great things God is doing for others around us, we should rejoice in the name of the Lord because He is showing Himself to be visible in our neighborhood. This is precisely the moment when we need to be determined in prayer and supplication, remaining extremely persistent in our faith. The sight of God blessing others should give you the strength and patience to endure and wait on God. This is exactly what the Canaanite woman observed, and she quickly said; "I see you, Lord; and I will thankfully take your crumbs." Do you see God? Will you accept His crumbs? Will you persist in your faith?

We must learn to endure in all circumstances and wait on the Lord with persistence of faith. In endurance, we make ourselves more than what we are, because we are reaching well beyond what is easily within our reach. With persistence of faith, we make enormous requests of the Lord because we know we serve an awesome, good and merciful God. We know He will make our cup overflow. *"You prepare a table before me in the presence of my enemies. You anoint my head with oil, my cup overflows."* (Psalm 23:5). You should never be satisfied with a half-filled cup, or even a full cup. You should always be willing to endure patiently until your cup over-flows, as you sit at the table God has prepared for you in the presence of your enemies. Do you have the vision of God that inspires you to wait on Him to prepare the great feast on your behalf? Beg God for His crumbs and watch how He will cause your cup to overflow. If you see yourself only as the person you believe you are, you make yourself less than what you really are. But, if you see yourself through the vision and purpose God has for your life, then you allow God to make you greater than what you are. If the Canaanite woman saw herself only as a Gentile, her request would not have been answered. But, because she was inspired by the vision of what God could do, and was persistent in her faith, God moved on her behalf in a mighty way. He will do the same for you, in the persistence of your faith.

Week 11 Day 5

THE ESSENCE
OF HOPE

"Let us hold unswervingly to the hope we profess, for he who promised is faithful.

—*HEBREWS 10:23*

G od always works it out on our behalf, in accordance to His will and purpose. He may not show up exactly when we think He should, but He is always right on time. God has complete dominion over time and space, so we can depend on His promises. Beware of weakening our hold on hope we profess by bringing our personal doubt or self-pity into the presence of the Lord and demanding an immediate response. God never fails, and we must not allow our hope in the Lord to fail due to a lack of endurance. The essence of hope is that we hold unswervingly faithful to what we profess unto the Lord. It is during the walk in the valley of death that we prove we are the chosen ones. God will work it out, if you have the patience and endurance to wait on His promise. Our Lord is faithful. Therefore, let your approach to God be along the line of "He Who promised is faithful."

A Call to Persevere: *"Therefore, brothers, since we have confidence to enter the Most Holy Place by the blood of Jesus, by a new and living way, opened for us through the curtain, that is, his body, and since we have a great priest over the house of God, let us draw near to God with a sincere heart in full assurance of faith."* (Verse 19-22). A sincere heart holds unswervingly to what the heart professes. In full assurance of faith is the essence of our hope in the Lord. All we need to do is hold on. Spiritual impatience is the most effectual obstacle to the promises of God, because it has a foundation built upon doubt and self-pity. You need to atone your doubt and self-pity with the Blood of Jesus. You cannot enter the Most Holy Place riding the sympathy train. God does not respond to your sympathy, but He is faithful to those who profess the name of the Lord and never lessens their grip on the hope identified by faith in Christ. Instead of holding on to the hope we profess, we tend to believe there are certain kind and virtuous things we should be able to enjoy without atoning them to Christ. When we do this, what we are really saying to God is that we do not trust Him with everything. This is hope in false pretense of faith. "Lord, I trust you; but I don't think I am going to turn over this one thing to you."

The Essence of Hope: *"Let us draw near to God with a sincere heart in full assurance to faith, having our hearts sprinkled to cleanse us from a guilty conscience and having our bodies washed with pure water."* (Verse 22). The essence of hope is we have been washed with the Blood of Jesus, reconciled to sin by the Atonement, and our hearts are cleansed of all guilt and wrongdoing toward the Lord and others. This all comes down to the quality of our relationship with Christ. It is in Christ that we are drawn nearer to God by the Holy Ghost intervening through intercessory prayer. The closer you are to Christ, the closer you will be to God. Faith and hope are strengthened to the degree of the close proximity within which we live our daily lives near the Cross of Christ. This closeness to Christ is what tightens our hold like a death grip to the faith we profess. Come close enough to the Lord to have your heart sprinkled by the Blood of Jesus and enter into the Kingdom of God with confidence and Blessed Assurance. Are you doubtful or faithful? Do you indulge in self-pity or hope? Have you been washed in the Blood of Jesus? Atone to Christ and draw near to God. That's the essence of hope in your faith in God.

Week 11 Day 6

JUDGEMENT IS NOW

"For it is time for judgment to begin with the family of God."

—*1 Peter 4:17*

We must understand that God works daily to put His House in order, so His judgment is on the saint every day. We serve in God's name. We love in God's name. We suffer in God's name. We are judged unto His Salvation, and that judgement is now. In sainthood, we must remember that salvation is a gift from God, not something we can request. Salvation is the great consideration of the Holy Ghost, not the result of living through a particular set of circumstances. Our experiences, whether in service, love or suffering, do not gain us salvation. Service, love and suffering are the portals through which salvation is poured into your soul. Do not speak of the portals, but rather preach the gospel of Jesus Christ into your soul and into the souls of others. It is the knowledge of the kingdom of God that brings us to the threshold of salvation. It is the judgement of God that determines if we receive the gift of stepping over the threshold into the procession of saints marching into the Kingdom. Salvation is not the result of proclaiming deliverance from pain and suffering, but the gift of receiving the Holy Spirit. Salvation is the good news that we must spread about God. Our service, love and suffering are wrapped in the good news. The right now judgement of God is along the very line of what we preach and teach about the Kingdom. Are you preaching the good news of God, or are you preaching your experiences?

Our life in Christ should never be about the experiences and blessings we receive. Our life in Christ should be about the life of Christ and how He lives in us. In spreading the good news about Christ Jesus, the judgement of God is always upon us. His judgement is a sign of the Father's love; for the Father chastises His children to grow up in the image of the Father, demonstrating His perfect character in service, love and suffering. Never indulge in self-pity if you find it difficult to connect to the Father's love. God is faithful, and His love never fails. You are to blame if you are not getting to God's love. You only need to present the truth of God in all His glory and honor, and the obstacles that are preventing you from getting to His love will be revealed. Once revealed, you must do the work to remove what is hindering you. You are judged right now, in every moment of every day, along the line of this specific work. Service, love and suffering in the name of God brings you expeditiously to His Throne of Judgement along the line of your obedience to the word of God.

There is never a good reason to be judged unfavorably by God. In your weakness and in your varied inabilities, God is at His strongest and greatest in your life. All you need to do is stand firm on the righteousness of the Lord, soaked in the Blood of the Lamb, proclaiming the Gospel of the Lord, God Almighty. In such a righteous and holy postulation, all hinderances to obedience are destroyed forthright. If God has willed anything or has purposed your life for a particular service, love or suffering, then He has the power to guarantee it will come to fruition. The judgement of God falls favorably on those who have destroyed every ounce of self-reliance and have abandoned themselves to Christ. God favors those whose heart is right, soul is righteous, and thoughts are pure. This is the very line along which we are judged right now, every day.

Week 11 Day 7

CONFESS AND BELIEVE

"That if you confess with your mouth, 'Jesus is Lord,' and believe in your heart that God raised him from the dead, you will be saved."

—Romans 10:9

There is no particular work, no mountain to climb, no person or place you can go to, nor any deed that can be accomplished under the heavens that will allow you to gain salvation. Salvation comes strictly by way of an utterance of the mouth and a belief of the heart—a confession and a belief. That's it! If you believe there is any other process by which you can be saved, then you are deadly mistaken. Your eternal life depends solely on your understanding of the divine order that the only way to the kingdom is the route that runs center to the life, death, resurrection, and ascension of Christ. Your good works, your fabulous achievements, your wondrous intellect, your brilliant mind, your electrifying personality, nor your great intentions, have no power to save your soul. Have you confessed with your mouth, "Jesus is Lord?" Do you believe in your heart that He was sent down from heaven in the flesh, suffered, crucified, raised and now sits on the right hand of the Throne of God?

"Christ is the end of the law so that there may be righteousness for everyone who believes." (Romans 10:4). Not birthright, not family name, not position in the church, but only righteousness in relationship to God leads to salvation in the Lord. We are no longer subjected to the laws handed down through Moses, but rather, we are saved by the Blood of the Lamb. Salvation is the result of the Power of the Redemption. Christ Jesus wiped away all our sins and placed our eternal lives in the power of His Resurrection. It was the word of God that was resurrected from the earthly tomb of Christ, not His body. The word lives in Christ Jesus, and if He lives in us, then the word of God is alive in us. "Draw near to God." It is through the living word that abides in Christ Jesus that we are given the knowledge and the path of righteousness to the Throne of Christ, when His Word abides in us. It is these very words that must be in our mouth and heart if we are to be saved, sanctified and filled with the Holy Ghost.

"The word is near you; it is in your mouth and in your heart." (Romans 10:8).

"Everyone who calls on the name of the Lord will be saved." (Romans 10:13). The righteousness by which we gain access to the procession of saints into the kingdom is not gained by eloquently quoting scripture. Holiness is not in singing the gospel, nor is favor given to the kind at heart. There is also no heaven or hell in a sin. Heaven and hell are in your mouth and in your heart. What is in your heart, and what comes out of your mouth? God hears our call and sees into our heart. He listens for our confessions and awaits evidence of our belief. Be vigilant in calling on the name of the Lord and be resolute in your belief that Christ died for your sins and now sits with His Father in heaven. Salvation is in your mouth and in your heart. It is nowhere else on earth or in heaven. Let the Word of God through Christ Jesus abide in you, and you in the Word, and you will be saved.

THE YOKE OF THE GOSPEL

"These are the Scriptures that testify about me, yet you refuse to come to me to have life."

—JOHN 5:39-40

The Scriptures were written by men to introduce the Gospel, to reveal the Life of Jesus Christ to the world; yet we tend to be yoked to the written words of men, rather than being yoked to the Life of Christ to whom the Scriptures reveal. If you are solely yoked to written words about Christ and not Christ Himself, the best you can ever do is develop a deep opinion of the Savior. No matter how deep your thoughts are concerning the Scriptures, written words will not give you life. You must become yoked by the "Come to Me" of Christ Jesus to have eternal life. Spiritually believing in Christ does not end with the last written word of the Scriptures. Believing in the Lord extends well beyond your opinion of the written words of men and deep into the abyss of eternity as you take on the perfect standards of Jesus to align your thoughts, beliefs, and soul. Christ is the standard, not Scriptures. God does not ask us to believe in the Bible, we are asked to believe in the Life of Christ. We are to take on the yoke of the Gospel and wear it with the standards of the Son of man. We are called to manifest freedom through the Gospel of Christ, not to exercise our free-will toward the extremities of our opinions. If we are freed through the perfect standards of Christ, then we will bring others to Christ along that same line; and Christ Himself, not the Scriptures, will dominate our lives. It will be Christ Who fills our mouth and heart.

The perfect standards of Christ are the only instrument by which, we as Christians, measure ourselves. We are not to measure ourselves by the standards or the opinions of others; nor are we to ask others to measure themselves by the standards of our opinions. Christ is the standard, not human opinion. There is no greater love than the Love of Christ. Jesus Christ will save your soul and give you eternal life. There is no power in the Scriptures, beyond revealing that Jesus Christ is the only Superhero you should be looking for. Irrespective of what has been written, you must believe Christ lived, died, and was raised from the dead. Without consideration or opinion, you must believe Christ ascended to the right hand of the Throne of God. This is the knowledge of the Gospel that you must get yoked-up with. Bow your soul only to the yoke of Jesus Christ and be vigilant to ensure that the yoke of the Gospel is the only yoke you introduce to the souls of others.

Be careful not to hinder Christ from having His way with others. Don't give others your opinion; give them the knowledge of the truth of Jesus Christ and let Christ work out the rest. Never make others feel they must see God through your eyes. Let everyone see God as God presents Himself to them. Beware of offering others any other yoke, other than the yoke of the Gospel of Jesus Christ. Also, beware that you, as well, do not consider anything other than being rightly connected to the perfect standards of the Lord. There is only one name by which we can be saved, that name is Jesus. Abide in Christ, and ensure Christ abides in you. Confess Jesus as Lord, believe in your heart in the Gospel, wear the yoke of the perfect standards of Christ around your neck, the crown of righteousness on your head, and never remove them.

OVERCOMING YOUR TEMPTATIONS

*"Then Jesus was led by the Spirit into
the desert to be tempted by the devil."*

—MATTHEW 4:1

Jesus was led by the Spirit into the desert, where He fasted for 40 days. When He was physically, mentally, and emotionally at His weakest, the Devil came and tempted Him with food. The Devil knew Jesus would be weak, because he was well-aware Jesus had not eaten in over a month. Imagine not eating for 40 days and there is no food in sight. This was the situation with Jesus. And just like the situation with Jesus, the Devil knows our weaknesses as well. The Devil knows our habits and addictions. As soon as you are led by the Spirit into your wilderness of denying yourself the things that bring you pleasure in the name of the Lord, Satan will wait until you are at your weakest moment and offer you a generous bribe or devise an unsuspecting scheme to catch you off guard. Whatever your addiction might be, whether it is gluttony, lust, greed, jealousy or anger, the Devil knows how to tempt you. He uses others that know you best and sends them under the guise of love and affection. He causes you and your spouse to be at odds with one another so he can tempt one of you to seek comfort in the arms of someone outside of your marriage.

Satan convinces us that we are wasting our time trying to be happy with someone we know God blessed us with, and overtime, he waits until the most opportune time to tempt us with food, riches, happiness and prestigious positions. Satan knows when we are lonely and depressed. He knows when we are brokenhearted. He knows every detail of our grandest dreams and most tantalizing desires. He shows up with a basket filled with trinkets. He knows you have a taste for alcohol. He knows when you have a man addiction or a woman fetish. The Devil knows you better than you know yourself. And when you least expect it, he shows up. He may show up offering a nice trip to a tropical island or promising to fulfill your greatest hopes and dreams. He may show up looking like a supermodel or like superman. So, beware of the Devil and his schemes to get you to turn away from God and forfeit your life in Christ. It may be a co-worker tempting you to anger; don't do it. It could be an old relationship tempting you to step outside of your marriage; don't give in. It may be a family member that offers you a drink, a smoke or another of your old vices; don't let them cause you to go to hell. Stand strong in your convictions and remain rightly related to the perfect character of Christ.

"If your right eye causes you to sin." We are not spiritually strong enough to deal with the Devil. Christ was able to overcome the temptations of Satan because Christ had the spiritual fortitude required to go up against the Devil, and to win. In fact, Christ fights the Devil on our behalf. Christ Jesus went down into Hades, fought Satan and took the keys to the Heavenly realm away from Satan, so Satan could not travel between universes wreaking havoc. We overcome our temptations by the strength of Christ abiding in us and us abiding in Christ. We put on the full armor of God to protect ourselves from the onslaught of the Devil. The Devil is the most patient being in the universe and will wait forever to catch you in a weak moment. He will wait an entire lifetime, if He has to. He'll lurk around endlessly just to get you to take a drink of whatever might put you back into battling that drinking addiction or tempt you to return to any other addictions.

If your problem is your right eye, God says pluck it out. If it is your right leg, God says cut it off. God says cut people off as well, if they tempt you to sin. Gods says it is better to be a lamed, one-eyed, friendless person in heaven than a popular supermodel in hell.

THE LULL OF IMPATIENCE

*"Where there is no revelation, the
people cast off restraint; but blessed
is he who keeps the law."*

—*Proverbs 29:18*

There is a spiritual difference between a natural interest and revelation from God. Revelations are born of God's spiritual inspiration; natural interests are born of man's own free-will. When we are spiritually inspired by the visions sent down from heaven, we are disciplined in our devotion, prayer and giving thanks. But when we have no vision from God, when revelations are not forthcoming, we become impatient with the lack of clear guidance from the Lord. Without the endurance to wait on the next spiritual insight, we are lulled by our impatience to become undisciplined in our prayer life. We relax spiritually and open ourselves up to temptation. We cast out the restraints of God's commands and sink back down into our iniquities. If we allow our impatience to open us up to temptation, we start to run with our own ideals, thoughts and desires. The grip of the word of God is loosened on our souls. Beware of the word of God loosening its grip, because we become open targets to the Devil's onslaught of temptation. The lull of impatience causes the relaxing of restraints, which leads to sin. When you begin to succumb to your own ideals, you very rarely do anything meaningful for God. Spiritual unproductivity, in and of itself, is a sin. Doing nothing is disrespectful to the pain and suffering that Christ endured on our behalf. We have a responsibility to the Redemption to honor the life, death, resurrection, and ascension of Christ. The greatest show of honor is spiritual endurance to keep all spiritual restraints attached to our soul, and to wait on the Lord until He speaks. This is a responsibility and a spiritual duty that should never experience neglect. The Devil should never be given access to the temple of God simply because we are impatient. We are right that God is good and merciful, but we still have a responsibility to uphold the law. When we loosen the restraints and ask God to prove His goodness and mercy, or when we find ourselves overcome with the temptations of sin, we are testing God; and God is not to be tested. *"Do not put the Lord your God to the test."* (Matthew 4:7). Do not test the Lord our God; and do not allow His goodness and mercy to be the reason you don't do your spiritual duty of upholding the law.

When there is revelation and spiritual vision from heaven, there is spiritual restraint and holy fortitude, as it is the vision which inspires us to make use of our lives on behalf of the Lord. Revelation incentivizes both our moral and spiritual character toward the duties of Christianity and holiness. So, beware of the lull of your impatience, earthly ideals, and personal interests. Test everything to ensure you are inspired by visions from heaven, and not temptations from the underground. Keep what is good and quickly discard anything that hinders you from your responsibility to the Cross. Your reach should always extend up to the heavens. If you have no vision of heaven, then you don't know the purpose of the stars. If you feel there is no revelation at hand, simply go amidst the darkness, look up to heaven and become inspired by the stars. The stars are auspicious signs that God rules the universe, and He is coming back. Seek no greater inspiration than to reach up to the hills, that's where your help comes from. Keep your spiritual wits about yourself, for the Devil is always seeking a way to get into your soul. Do not allow your soul to be the Devil's playground. Keep sight of God; for the Lord is always visible in the sun, the moon and the stars. The saint must *"pray constantly, give thanks in all circumstances, do not worry,"* and never be lulled by impatience.

Week 12 Day 4

THE GIFT OF PATIENCE

"I am coming soon. Hold on to what you have, so that no one will take your crown."

—*REVELATIONS 3:11*

John wrote to the Church in Philadelphia to "Hold on!" In this context, "Hold on" means to endure in the face of extreme circumstances. God knows the challenges we face and the lull of impatience we are prone to succumb to. Through John, God sends us a message to be patient, and our endurance will be rewarded with the crown of the Glory of God. "Hold on" is a manner of patience that is much more than simple endurance. The life of a faithful servant of God through Christ is in the hands of God. You never know how God intends to use you in His service, but God knows that His will and purpose for your life places extreme pressure and strain on your moral character and spiritual endurance. And there are times when the servant of the Lord says, "I don't think I can hold on any longer." God does not yield to your doubt or concerns; He keeps the pressure on until His purpose is fulfilled in you. Once His purpose is satisfied, you will receive your crown. The crown of the Glory of God is the gift for your patience and endurance in the midst of God's pressure and strain, even when you don't think you can last another second, "Hold on!" Know that you can patiently trust your life to the hands of God. God never fails, and His love endures forever. The patience of faith in God is the bedrock of your relationship with Christ Jesus. Hold on to your faith, no matter the pressure and the strain, and make sure no one takes your crowning glory, which is in the Lord.

Patience with faith is not a weak human sentiment, but rather a strong spiritual trustfulness built upon your relationship with Christ. It connects you to God's love, goodness, and mercy. Though God is stretching your faith beyond limits, and even though you do not know His will and purpose, you do know that God is faithful. He is the same faithful God of Abraham, Isaac, and Jacob. He is the same God that saved Jonah from the belly of a whale. Like Jonah, you may be thrown overboard into the stormy sea of your extreme circumstances, when you are not rightly related to the eternal truth that God is love, He is good, and He's merciful. Faith is the cornerstone of your patience, patience fuels endurance and gives you the confidence that you can trust in the Lord. Patience is a gift from the Holy Spirit; it is the gift that keeps on giving and keeps you standing on the word of God. For what other good is your patience?

God's only interest is that we choose an eternal life with Him through completely abandoning ourselves to Christ. Complete abandonment requires a level of faith that is not easily reached. We must stretch well beyond ourselves to get to the level of faith that gives us complete confidence in God. Many of us are not quite there yet. There are places in our lives that faith has not touched; places where faith cannot reach; places where we still fall to temptation. This is precisely why God applies His pressure and strain to our lives. God is constantly stretching our faith beyond what is humanly possible, beyond what is easily within our grasp, to get us to the point where we can have patience in all situations He brings us to. God really does want us to receive our crown. His sincerity is in the fact that He sent Christ to die on the Cross for our sins; so, we would have the opportunity to receive the crown of the Glory of His Kingdom. All that He asks is that we "Hold on" with patience, endurance, and faith that He will deliver on His promises.

TAKE RESPONSIBILITY FOR YOUR OWN SPIRIT

"Make every effort to add to your faith goodness; and to goodness, knowledge; and to knowledge, self-control; and to self-control, perseverance; and to perseverance, godliness, and to godliness, brotherly kindness; and to brotherly kindness, love."

—2 PETER 1:5-7

We are called by the glory and goodness of God through His divine nature. Divine means it is not born of the human spirit, but of the Spirit of God. Through the knowledge of the Divine Spirit of God we are given the gift of faith. Beyond the gift of faith, we must be responsible for our own spirit. Our spirit is subject to the onslaught of evil desires that tempt us to become corrupt in our heart. If your heart is corrupt, you cannot "participate in the divine nature of the great and precious promises" of the Lord. Therefore, you must "escape the corruption in the world caused by evil desires." (Verse 4). For this reason, you must take upon yourself the yoke of the perfect character of Christ Jesus. To the gift of faith, you must add goodness, knowledge, self-control, perseverance, godliness, brotherly kindness, and love. To "add" means there is something we must take responsibility for. God has a part, as there are things we cannot do; we have a part, and there are things God cannot do for us. What God cannot do are the things we must take responsibility for ourselves. God cannot give us the perfect character of Christ; these are the characteristics we must develop and add to our character. For example, if we have an addiction to alcohol, over consumption leads to corruption of the heart and spirit. Therefore, we must add to our character self-control over our corrupt addictions. Corrupt addictions are the result of not being able to escape the corruption in the world caused by deadly evil desires: sexual lust, hatred, jealousy, greed, anger, bitterness, spiritual laziness and gluttony.

God will not give us self-control, a good nature or good habits. He also will not give us good character. These are things we should want for ourselves and must take the responsibility to develop. Salvation is our responsibility to work out. God gifts to us salvation, but we must work it out to develop our own character, discipline and habits of doing the things we do. Taking the initiative can be a daunting task, but we must do it. God is not going to do it for us. You are completely wasting your time testing God, if you believe God is going to show up and work goodness, knowledge, self-control, perseverance, godliness, brotherly kindness, and love into your character. That's your responsibility. You must have some spiritual sweat equity in building your relationship with God through Christ. God has done His part; now you must do yours.

Beware of holding on to the notion of free-will through the exercise of your God-given volition. Yes, you have a right to yourself and your own self-interests, but you must give up that right to follow Jesus. You must escape the grip of self-doubt and stop hesitating in taking the initiative. The initiative starts with denying yourself the right to yourself. Hesitation, doubt and refusal to take the initiative puts you at risk of losing God's favor and damaging your position in God's grace. Take the responsibility for your own spirit; step into faith by moving to the other side of the river, away from your inequities, evil desires, and temptations; then burn the bridge down so you can't go back across. You may have to leave some people behind, and that's okay. It is better to lose some friends and gain the great and precious promises in the divine nature of God. Get into the habit of asking; "God, what's your interests?" Take the initiative where you are today, not where you want to be tomorrow.

Week 12 Day 6

IF YOU DON'T HAVE LOVE, YOU DON'T HAVE ANYTHING

"If I give all I possess to the poor and surrender my body to the flames, but have not love, I gain nothing."

—1 Corinthians 13:3

1 Corinthians 13:13 says; *"And now these three remain: faith, hope and love. But the greatest of these is love."* Love is the

bedrock and the cornerstone, the foundation and the support structure, by which all relationships are built. Without love, you have nothing. Love is not a definitive concept for most of us, because we really don't know what love is about, or what we mean when we say we love. This causes the feeling of love to be fleeting at times. One day you are head-over-heels in love with a person, and the next day you are not. Love can be described as the supreme feeling that controls our emotional output and practical actions toward another person. From the spiritual perspective, Jesus demands that He is the single Supreme Being to whom we utmost prefer to give our love to. We should love nothing or no one more than we love Jesus. "If anyone comes to me and does not hate his father and mother, his wife and children, his brothers and sisters – yes, even his own life – he cannot be my disciple." (Luke 14:26). God is a jealous God, and when the Holy Ghost sheds the love of God in our hearts, God intends for Christ Jesus to be first-in-line to receive the greatest share of the output from our hearts. Jesus must come first in our hearts, and everything and everyone else must have an inferior position in our lives. This is the one demand of Christ where He offers no compromise. If you don't have love for Christ first, you don't have anything.

When the Holy Ghost sheds the love of God in my heart, the first thing I realize is that God loves me, even though I am unworthy of His love. The knowledge of God's sovereign love for a wretch like me throws all previous spiritual assumptions and religious predispositions out the window. God does not love us because we are lovable; for we are not. He loves us because it is His Divine nature to do so. There is absolutely nothing we can do to earn God's love; it is solely a gift of the Holy Spirit. But now, the Holy Spirit says I should show others the same level of love I have been shown. I must "love as I have been loved." I must love every person God brings into my purview and within my path, even those I don't like, respect or care for. Matthew 22:39 says; *"Love your neighbor as yourself"* is God's second greatest command. The greatest command is to love God Himself with all your heart. 2 Peter 1:7 says to add *"to brotherly kindness, love."* To exhibit this manner of love requires a deep love of Christ. To love someone who hates you or intends to cause you harm requires a spiritual touch. A touch that the human heart does not naturally produce. Only the Holy Ghost can impart the foundational love of God that allows you to develop the discipline toward the perfect character of Christ, which in turn gives you the ability to love your enemy. In essence, you must take on the Divine nature of God in order to love like God does. If you don't take on God's nature, you cannot love others like God loves you. This is not a love you can approach casually nor by wading in the shallow end of the river. You must dive head-first into the deepest portion of the river, with faith and hope.

WITH SIMPLE INTENTIONS

"For if you possess these qualities in increasing measure, they will keep you from being ineffective and unproductive in your knowledge of our Lord Jesus Christ."

—*2 Peter 1:8*

When we are intentional with our actions, we are conscious of what we are doing. There are moments when we are conscious of growing our knowledge of our Lord Jesus Christ; but these are fleeting moments. We must work daily with conscious intent to add good qualities to our character like those mentioned in Peter. We must consciously focus until we are effective and productive in growing our knowledge of God. "Possessing these qualities in increasing measure" should never become an unconscious habit; our thirst for Christ should always be intentional and without ceasing. If we pause our pursuit of our Lord Jesus Christ, we risk becoming spiritual slugs. The proper approach to developing the perfect character of Christ in increasing measure, is to remain intentionally effective and productive, conscious at all times, until the life of Christ Jesus totally consumes your life. When this happens, you will eat, sleep and drink Jesus. Christ will be manifested in everything you do. When you have added all the qualities of Christ Jesus, your hands will have the touch of God. Your relationship with Christ will eventually become the easiest and simplest relationship you have. If you are not there, keep your every intention toward Christ Jesus simple and consciously increase the measure of His perfect qualities in your own character.

Beware of evolving into a habitual Christian. Do you pray by habit? Perhaps attending church is a Sunday morning ritual of yours. What about Bible Study on Wednesdays and Prayer Meeting on Thursdays? Anytime you attempt to make your practice of Christianity a habit, God will interrupt your spirituality and drive your soul into a valley of introspection. Reading the Bible daily is not productive if it is done out of habit. The Bible is just a collection of words if read out of habit, but it comes to life once you realize the Bible is about the knowledge of our Lord Jesus Christ; and the Bible is only a portal into the life of Christ. True knowledge of Christ Jesus comes from having simple intentions with no interests greater than your interests for the Lord. God will destroy your habits of practicing Christianity if they are ineffective and unproductive in increasing your knowledge of Christ. God intends for us to worship Christ, not worship the habits of worshipping Christ. With simple intentions toward Christ Jesus, we are to possess His perfect qualities. To take on the character of Christ, Christ has to abide in me and me in Him, not simply the ability to quote scripture as a habit. I must love Jesus intentionally. When I learn to love Jesus intentionally, I can then offer others the same intentional love. I can then add to my character, with increasing measure, the qualities of Christ. Intentional love for Christ, and others, means there is visible evidence of spiritual inspiration, and no indication that love is habit-driven. Acting intentionally will eventually lead you to unconscious fruitfulness in your spirituality. The things you are conscious of are the areas requiring growth. If you are conscious of prayer, then you need to grow in your prayer life until you are no longer conscious of it. If you are conscious of your righteousness, then you need to grow in your righteousness. If there is any place where you are conscious, let God in intentionally and let Him work that thing out.

Week 13 Day 1

WITH CLEAR CONSCIENCE

*"So I strive always to keep my conscience
clear before God and man."*

—ACTS 24:16

O ur conscience is the supernatural essence of our spirit
through which God connects with us. Our conscience
has a natural tendency to connect with the deepest regions of
our soul and highest peak of our mental ability. Conscience
pulls us deeper and higher into ourselves and into the knowledge of God. When God says, "Come higher," He is speaking
to our conscience. To the degree we are connected to the call

of God, our conscience is clear. With a clear conscience we are able to embrace the commands of our Lord and clearly detect whether God is calling us to go deeper or higher. Conscience connects us to God in accordance to God's calling and in accordance to what He has purposed our lives for but understand there must be a connection. We must decide if we will answer the call and if we are sure about the direction we are pulled toward. What is your conscience telling you? Is your conscience clear? Are you called to go deeper or climb higher? If I have the pure intentions of looking into the face of God, without regard to my own self-interests, my conscience will always connect me to the perfections of God's commands and pull me into the proper direction that my life should go. The only question that needs to be answered is "Will I go?" I must strive to always keep my conscience so clear that I will walk simply with the intentions of pleasing God, and I will make my intentions clear to others around me; that my eyes are only fixed on the glory of the Lord.

God makes His commands through the life of Jesus Christ that is in us. While these commands are harsh and extremely difficult to obey, the very instance we take on the Divine nature of spiritual obedience, His commands become simple and easy. Taking on God's Divine nature requires a clear conscience and spiritual intention toward obedience. Are you intent on being obedient? Your spiritual intent toward obedience should pull your soul deeper into sympathy with the tragedy of the Cross of Christ. Your clear conscience and the Divine nature of God abiding in you should give you clear direction concerning "what is good and pleasing and perfect in God's eyes." God does not command imperfection; rather, He commands that we are perfect in character and disposition of the heart's love. *"Do not conform to the pattern of this world but be transformed by the renewing of your mind."* (Romans 12:2). The none-conformity spoken of in Romans comes from having a clear conscience before God and man. I must make a conscious effort to walk intentionally aligned with God in such a manner, that I don't crucify Jesus unconsciously over and over again.

The manner to which we respect the Cross of Christ is by keeping our conscience clear before God and man, so that we remain completely open to God's spiritual pull on our life and obey without question or doubt. When there is doubt, my conscience is not clear and my connection to God through the life of Christ is suspect. God has made His expectations clear. Do I have a conscience that allows me to be rightly connected to God's will? Am I so tuned in to God's voice that I hear even His slightest utterance, down to His lowest whisper, that I know without a doubt what He is asking me to do? The Holy Ghost does not strike with thunder; His touch is slight and gentle. Don't mistake it for the blowing of the wind. Keep your conscience clear before God and Man, and your connection to His will right and proper.

GET THE CONTENTION OUT

*"We always carry around in our body
the death of Jesus, so that the life of Jesus
may also be revealed in our body."*

—2 CORINTHIANS 4:10

We must commit to intentionally walking every day in a spiritual manner through which others can see the goodness of God's grace upon our lives. We should consider ourselves walking billboards, faithfully advertising the life of Jesus Christ and everything He has done for us. Everything about us, our walk, our talk, our intellectual output, our mental contemplations, our personal interactions, our private thoughts, and our public displays should exude and exalt the life of Christ. As a saint, when others see you, they should instantly notice the difference in your conscious life in Christ, and the difference should be easily identified as the manifestation of the Life of Christ. The Life of Christ will be revealed in your flesh when the Death of Christ abides in your body. What prevents us from carrying around the Death of Christ in our body? There are things God expects from us that we refuse to accept responsibility for; therefore, we deny Jesus. If we deny Jesus in any aspect of our lives, then we are not carrying around His Death in our body. If I allow my flesh to lust sexually and indulge in my own self-interests concerning other sinful desires, I am refusing to abandon myself to Christ Jesus. These become the points of contention between Christ and myself, and I am not carrying the Death of Christ in my body when there is contention with His clear expectations of my life. I must get the contention out before the Life of Jesus can be revealed in my daily walk. I must get past my contention with the commands of God. "Your will Lord, not mine!" The instant I deny myself and obey God, the contention disappears, and the Life of Christ is manifested in my life, as I walk in the Light of the Glory of Jesus Christ.

There must be no contention between my interests and the interests of God. The very moment I decide to walk in the light of the glory, our Lord Jesus Christ steps into the midst of my circumstances and works out all the contention. But, if I insist upon keeping up the contention, I crucify our Lord over and over again. I must allow the Atonement and Redemption to keep me so connected to Jesus that there is never a point of contention, disagreement, or doubt. Disagreement and doubt have a way of driving a wedge between me and my King. If there is a gap between Jesus and me, I am weakened spiritually, and the Devil will have access to my spirit. I must remain spiritually strong and rightly connected with my Savior. If not, I will eventually sink into a valley of seeking sympathy from others and indulge in self-pity. Self-pity causes contention to grow. God engineers our circumstances on our behalf as a means of showing just how marvelous, merciful and magnificent He is. God allows our hearts to be broken so He can prove just how invincible we are through His goodness and grace. Get the contention out and let God manifest the riches of His precious promises in your mortal flesh. Don't you dare get down on Jesus. Lift Christ up, and He will take you higher than your mind can imagine. God has complete power and dominion over your circumstances. If He has placed you there, get into spiritual alignment with the Life of Christ, for God has put you there for a powerful reason. Get spiritually prepared and stay prepared. Spiritual strength keeps the contention out and the word of God active in your life. It's done in such a manner that it allows the Life of Christ to be revealed in everything you are about.

PARTICIPATE IN THE ABUNDANCE

*"Through these he has given us his very
great and precious promises, so that
through them you may participate in
the divine nature and escape corruption
in the world caused by evil desires."*

—*2 PETER 1:4*

"*N*o eye has seen, no ear has heard, no mind has con-
ceived what God has prepared for those who love him."
(1 Corinthians 2:9). While we are made to participate in
it, the human mind cannot begin to imagine the breadth,

height, width and depth of God's abundance. It is through the Divine nature of God that we gain access to His great and precious promises. Once the Holy Ghost imparts God's nature in us, we then must work the Divine nature into our human nature before God can reveal all that He has prepared for us. We take on God's Divine nature by intentional acts, and the instant we receive God's nature, we immediately recognize His abundance. When we love God, there is absolutely nothing we could ever want that is beyond His enormous capacity. We are the children of the Most-High King of Kings. There is nothing the King of Kings cannot afford to give His children. We are not here to simply conquer and overcome struggle. God's desire is that we all strive in His Divine nature and enjoy the abundance that He makes available to His children. We are more than conquerors through Christ, the Lord. As Oswald Chambers states: "God will tax the last grain of sand and the remotest star to bless us if we will obey Him." That is one of the great and precious promises of God. We cannot imagine all that God has prepared for us. We walk around as if God has forsaken us or cut us off from our inheritance. The love of God for His children never fails. If you have not received your inheritance or access to the abundance of the great and precious promises, then you have not done your part. God is ready to bless you the very moment you are ready to abandon yourself to Him in total obedience. God never promised us things would be easy. Not every road He places our feet on will be paved in gold. There will be struggle and strife. Why should we not suffer? We caused Jesus' suffering. Don't indulge in the "Woe is me!" Be joyful always, pray without ceasing and give thanks irrespective of your circumstances. Any other attitude in life blocks you from participating in the riches of the grand inheritance of the glory of the kingdom of God. "Yes, Lord! For the rest of my days!"

"Woe is me!" is the giving of a sinful nature that runs counter to the Divine nature of God. Self-pity is a sin that blocks you from participating in the tiniest of God's abundance. Self-pity is the foundation of self-interest. God does not allow us to come before His throne in a self-interested nature. We can only approach His throne after we have worked His Divine nature into our human nature, making ourselves one with the Divine. Until we have taken on God's nature, we are simply spiritual beggars selfishly chasing after God's blessings. God demands that we chase after Him, and Him only, then all else will be given to us, in exceeding abundance. You will know when you have entered into the right relationship with God, because you will see no value in material wealth, but rather understand that all good and precious things are drawn from the wisdom well of God's gracious promises. If you are not participating in God's abundance, grace, favor, promises, power, and exceeding joy, God says that is a "you issue." He has done His part. He has given you His Divine nature. The rest is up to you; for His great abundance awaits your participation.

Week 13 Day 4

HE'S COMING BACK

"And if I go and prepare a place for you,
I will come back and take you to be with
me that you also may be where I am."

—*John 14:3*

"I will come back" are the words of comfort Jesus offered His disciples. The words are also the capstone of His Transfiguration at Gethsemane. "I will come back" confirmed that Jesus had committed Himself to His Father to go into Jerusalem to suffer and die on the Cross for our sins. "I will come back" also shows that Jesus knew He would be resurrected from the grips of death. "I will come back" was a forecast that He would ascend into Heaven and sit at the right hand of the Throne of God, with all power in His hands. And it is with this power that He is coming back to take us with Him, back up to Heaven. "In my Father's House are many rooms." The Life, Death, Resurrection, and Ascension of Jesus Christ are all the precursors to His "I will come back and take you to be with Me." Jesus' disciples struggled with that statement because they could not fully comprehend what Jesus was saying. They knew His Life from walking with Him. They knew His Way from talking with Him. They knew His Truth from learning from Him. But His disciples had no congenial experiences to help them comprehend spiritually what was to come in the events that followed the Transfiguration at Gethsemane. The nature of the human spirit is incapable of cognizing the events of the Cross, Resurrection, and Ascension. Therefore, we cannot naturally conceive He's coming back. What does it really mean that Jesus is coming back? It means we also must go through a spiritual transfiguration; there must be a renewing of our spirit. It means we also must bear the Cross; the death of Christ must be in our bodies. It means we must also experience our own death and resurrection; we must die mortally so that our spirits can rise up. When Jesus comes back, He will take the spirits of those who love Him back with Him so we can be with Him in Heaven.

Jesus has already prepared a place for us. *"I am going there to prepare a place for you."* (Verse 2). Jesus rose from the grave with the power to give eternal life, and He ascended into Heaven giving access to His Throne to anyone who wants to follow. Don't miss the significance of His Ascension following His Resurrection. Jesus did not have to die for us. He chose to do so; it was His choice. He chose to obey His Father. If He had ascended into Heaven following His Transfiguration, He would not have been much more than an historical celebrity to the world. But He came down off the Mount of Olives, out of the garden of Gethsemane, and rode into Jerusalem, agonizing over His Death, on the back of a donkey. Because He suffered and was crucified, God was able to raise Him from the dead and place all power in His hands. His power is the result of His obedience to His Father. Jesus chose to self-identify with the wretched, destitute and brokenhearted, instead of basking in His own glory. Now, He is telling us that He's coming back to take us where we can live with Him through eternity. But, in telling us He's coming back, He is also telling us to get prepared for His second coming.

Jesus is not coming back as the Son of God. In His second coming, He is coming back as the King of Kings, with all power and all-knowing and all presence. As the result of His Death, Resurrection, and Ascension, He is now the Lord of Lords. Rest assuredly in this knowledge and get yourself prepared.

ARE YOU READY?

*"You know the way to the place
where I am going."*

—*John 14:4*

"I *am the way and the truth and the life. No one comes to the
Father except through me."* (John 14:6). We know Jesus is
coming back, and we know the way to the Kingdom of God,
but are we ready? It is one thing to have knowledge, but it is
altogether something else to be ready. To be ready implies
you have prepared yourself. Knowledge is worthless until you
apply it to your practical actions. You can have knowledge of
the word of God, but having the ability to quote scripture is
meaningless without the ability to live the word. You can be

ordained to teach the word, but no one is ordained to live the word. You can be given a gift from God, but you still must put in the work to get ready to ascend into Heaven. Life is no fairytale. While God intends for this life to be simple, He does not intend for it to be easy until we come into perfect union with Him through His Son, Christ Jesus. Are you ready to obey Jesus? Jesus is the only portal by which we walk through the pearly gates. Do you believe Jesus was the Son of God? Do you believe He was crucified, and God raised Him from the dead? Do you believe He ascended into Heaven and sits on the right hand of the Throne of God with all power in His Hands? And do you love Christ Jesus? Your love of Christ is the first act of becoming spiritually fit, getting yourself ready, for the kingdom.

"If anyone loves me, he will obey my teachings. My Father will love him, and we will come to him and make our home with him." (John 14:23). Loving Christ is not a simple utterance of; "I love you, Lord!" Your love for Christ is displayed in the form of obedience to Christ's teachings. Love is not displayed by simply going to church on Sunday, Bible study on Wednesday, prayer meeting on Thursday and Choir practice on Saturday. Love is a daily walk in obedience to the Throne and every word that emits from it. Obedience is not a convenience. Jesus could have conveniently gone up to Heaven glorified by grace from the Mount of Olives, but He turned His back on glory, and descended to the mountain, straight into His suffering, persecution and crucifixion. He obeyed His Father. We must deny ourselves and demonstrate the same

level of obedience in our love for Christ. Are you ready to show Jesus that you love Him? What do your daily actions, thoughts and desires tell Jesus about your love for Him? Are you spiritually fit for the Kingdom of God and all the glory of His great and precious promises? You must be prepared to bear your cross for Christ. You must love the Lord, just as He loved you when He died on the Cross for your sins.

"If anyone would come after me, he must deny himself and take up his cross daily and follow me." (Luke 9:23). We must live intentionally with the daily mindset that we are getting ourselves ready to meet our King. Imagine having knowledge of the fact that Jesus is coming back today around 12 o'clock noon. Imagine everything you would do to get yourself prepared for His coming. Imagine all the things you would suddenly deny yourself. Imagine all the things you would instantly stop doing and the things you would start doing. Imagine how frantic you would be concerning getting yourself ready to meet the King of Kings, the Lord of Lords. Whatever you imagine, those are the things you should be doing every moment of every day to get yourself ready. Get ready and stay ready for the Lord.

GET RIGHT WITH JESUS

"And why do you worry about clothes?
See how the lilies of the field grow."

—*Matthew 6:28*

When was the last time you took a good look at your life and really considered the things you worry about and the things you make a priority in your life? Think about all the nights you have gotten on your knees and prayed to God, asking Him to bring the right person into your life. Think about all the times you have asked God to bless you with a particular car, house, job or some other material possession. Now consider if you have ever thought about the lilies in the field, the birds in the air, the sun, the moon, and the stars. None of these things are conscious of what they are; they simply exist as they are. Birds don't pray for a companion. Lilies don't ask God for clothing; and the moon does not ask for anything. But they all exist in enormous splendor. Just like God knows that birds need to eat, and lilies need sunshine, He knows your every need as well. Not only does He know your every need, want and desire; God also loves you far greater than He loves a bird or a lily. God will adorn you with an even greater level of grandness than anything He has ever adorned in nature. All you have to do is get right with the Lord and simply exist as He made you. God is not asking you to be anything you are not. Just be the magnificent being He made you. Stop trying to be useful to God, and just get right with Jesus. The sun, moon, and the stars don't ask God to be useful; they just exist as the sun, moon, and the stars. They allow God to use them as He has purposed them. So, don't worry about where you live, what you drive, or what you wear; instead, focus on bringing yourself into right relationship with Jesus Christ. If you get yourself right with God, and just exist as He has made you, He will pour out blessings you can't even imagine. God knows you want a good man or a good woman. Get right with Jesus. God knows you want nice things and a great job. Get right with Jesus. God knows you want great friends and a nice house in a nice neighborhood. Get right with Jesus. If there is anything lacking in your life, get right with Jesus. Poor health? Get right with Jesus. Broken heart? Get right with Jesus.

Stop trying to make a deal with God. You have nothing to offer God, but your heart. Our Lord, God Almighty, wants you to have no conscious knowledge or desire concerning your usefulness to Him. If you believe God can use you, then He cannot use you. If you have no conscious interest in being used by God, then He can use you. All God wants you to do is to become one with Him through Christ, Who is one with God. It is in this oneness that all your worries are taken away. The birds and the lilies are one with God, because they simply exist for His glory. Exist only for the glory of God, and then watch how He will make rivers of living water flow into you and through you. The Spirit of God is the living water that will flow into you and create in you a spirit focused on nothing but pleasing Jesus. Even the sun, as powerful of an energy source as it is, shines to the will God. Likewise, let your light shine to the will of the Lord and get your soul rightly related with the perfect character of Jesus Christ. Don't you know that God knows the circumstances He has placed you in? Don't you realize He knows what He made you for? Just exist, and in your spiritual existence, rightly connected to Christ, you will be perfect in God's eyes, and only then will you be useful to Him. If you think there is a greater pair of eyes to appeal to, you are gravely mistaken. Get yourself right with Jesus and stop worrying. Do it now, and forever more.

THE LOVE THAT LIFTS YOU UP

"Who shall separate us from the love of Christ?
Shall trouble or hardship or persecution or
famine or nakedness of danger or sword?"

—ROMANS 8:35

"*F*or your sake we face death all day long; we are considered as sheep to be slaughtered." (Verse 36). God does not promise us a trouble-free life. In fact, He tells us we will have trials and tribulations in His name. But God also tells us that He has power and dominion over our circumstances, and Christ has overcome the world. Therefore, it doesn't matter the situation, condition or times you find yourself engulfed in; nothing can separate you from the love of God. Once you enter into holy communion with Christ, you have a bond with the Lord that cannot be broken. Paul is adamant when he says, "We are more than conquerors." Our troubles, heartaches, pain and sorrow are all designed to break us down to nothing, so we can get rightly connected to Christ. The very instance we cry out from the belly of our horrid circumstances, just as Jonah did from the belly of the whale, God begins to build us up spiritually and makes us stronger, better and more upright, holy and righteous. Our troubles are meant to push us down into spiritual poverty, the point to where life is meaningless without the Lord, and that is exactly the space where God does His greatness work. This low point is the very place where Christ takes hold of your hand and shows you just how good God is. Nothing keeps us from the love of God, but you must chase after your relationship with the Lord. The Lord is not going to chase you, but He will raise you out of your despair, complex issues, and feelings of abandonment and rejection from others. Christ will place your feet on solid ground and give you entrance to the express lane leading to the great and precious promises of His Father.

We are definitely more than conquerors. We are here to do much more than just overcome. We are meant to thrive in our existence with Christ. This is not some imaginary fairytale; this is God's promise to those who love Him. God's glory is not a place you can get to by bus, train or plane. God' glory is not in the box seats at the stadium or in the front row of the auditorium. In the midst of our troubles and hardships, Christ shows up and makes us the victor, the champion, and the rockstar. We don't get there because we are brave, handsome, intelligent, witty, intuitive, or courageous. The love of God, the intercessory prayer of the Holy Ghost, and the hand of Christ all work together to lift us up and make us superstars in the Kingdom. You may not think so, but the hands of Christ can reach you no matter where you are. Where you are right now is the right place at the right time. Your relationship with Christ is what gives you access to the Light of the Glory of the Kingdom of God, not how cleaned up you may think you need to be before coming to God. "Come as you are." Just call on His name, and rivers of living water will flow into you. Let God deal with what needs to change in your life. Completely abandon every thought that you need to change anything about your life before going to God. There is something special, extraordinary and magnificent that happens in the life of the saint who holds onto the love of Christ and Christ onto him or her. The love of God in Christ is a love that lifts you up, every time, out of every situation, out of every sorrow, out of every pain, out of every trouble and hardship.